Japanese Public Diplomacy in European Countries

To address the issue of the lack of integration and common policy among Japan's cultural promotion actors and institutions, Gadjeva explores an integrated approach for Japanese public diplomacy through public-private partnerships.

She examines the potential of the Japan Foundation as a central public diplomacy actor in Europe, facilitating a Public-Private Partnership Platform. Focusing on France and Bulgaria, Gadjeva observes the Japan Foundation's role, contributions, and activities implemented between the 1970s and 2018, both autonomously and in collaboration with Japanese and local public and private actors. She compares the Foundation's initiatives in the two countries, highlighting both the strong points and the space for improvement. In addition, Gadjeva points out essential Japanese, French, and Bulgarian actors with potential for future cooperation with the Japan Foundation through public-private partnerships. Drawing on her interviews with Bulgarian and French representatives, she examines the image of Japan and the future expectations from Japan. Revealing certain cultural aspects and less-explored areas of Japanese soft power, she proposes specific project proposals for integrated public diplomacy initiatives implemented through a Public-Private Partnership Platform facilitated by the Japan Foundation.

Providing valuable insights into the strong and insufficient points of Japan's public diplomacy in Europe and policy recommendations, this book will be of great interest to scholars and professionals in the spheres of Japanese public diplomacy, foreign cultural policy, and Japanese-European international relations.

Nadejda Gadjeva completed a bachelor's degree in global studies at the Akita International University in Japan, a one-year course in political studies at the Institut d'Etudes Politiques de Rennes (Sciences Po Rennes) in France, and master's and Ph.D. programs in international relations at the Ritsumeikan University in Japan. She explores the relations between Europe and Japan with a focus on public diplomacy and cultural diplomacy as instruments for increasing the regions' cultural presence and international partnerships. Nadejda Gadjeva has various publications in Japanese and European academic journals and has participated in academic conferences and symposiums in Japan.

Routledge Contemporary Japan Series

For more information about this series, please visit: *www.routledge.com/
Routledge-Contemporary-Japan-Series/book-series/SE0002*

Japanese Public Diplomacy in European Countries

The Japan Foundation in Bulgaria and France

Nadejda Gadjeva

LONDON AND NEW YORK

First published 2022
by Routledge
4 Park Square, Milton Park, Abingdon, Oxon OX14 4RN

and by Routledge
605 Third Avenue, New York, NY 10158

Routledge is an imprint of the Taylor & Francis Group, an informa business

British Library Cataloguing-in-Publication Data
A catalogue record for this book is available from the British Library

Library of Congress Cataloguing-in-Publication Data
A catalog record has been requested for this book

ISBN: 978-1-032-19353-3 (hbk)
ISBN: 978-1-032-19354-0 (pbk)
ISBN: 978-1-003-25879-7 (ebk)

DOI: 10.4324/9781003258797

Typeset in Times New Roman
by Apex CoVantage, LLC

Contents

1   Introduction

In the past, the most prevalent type of diplomacy was the traditional or classical diplomacy. It has been characterized as a direct and official communication between government officials of particular countries. In the 21st century, the nature of power has changed and the role of another type of diplomacy – public diplomacy – has been growing. Different from the traditional diplomacy, public diplomacy is an unofficial, indirect, and dialogic diplomacy, practiced by mixed coalitions of governmental, intergovernmental, and nongovernmental actors. In the international society, an increasing number of diplomats and political leaders consider public diplomacy a means for projecting a positive national image as well as for increasing their country's cultural presence abroad. It is also exercised with the aim of building long-term relationships among states and mutual trust that establish an enabling environment for government policies.

Japan is a country that puts a great emphasis on public diplomacy. It began to exercise it since the 1860s, the period when the country started its process of modernization (Ogawa, 2009, p. 272). Some of the first public diplomacy initiatives of Japan include its participation in World Expositions as well as particular public relations activities conducted during the Russo-Japanese War. After World War II, public diplomacy was applied to transform the prewar image of Japan as a militaristic country into a harmonious and peaceful democracy. Afterwards, in the late 1960s and the early 1970s, it was exercised in order to present Japan to the world as a technologically and economically advanced nation. At present, Japan's public diplomacy objectives evolved to include the establishment of prosperous international relations and a favorable environment for Japanese diplomacy.

Through the Public Diplomacy Department at the Ministry of Foreign Affairs, the Japan Foundation, the Cabinet Office, and other organizations and agencies, Japan exercises public diplomacy initiatives to increase its cultural presence and partnership with Europe. Despite the cultural activities of various public and private actors, the perception is that Japan's

DOI: 10.4324/9781003006251-1

presence in Europe has not yet reached its full potential. An audit conducted by the European Council on Foreign Relations (ECFR) indicated "scarceness of Japanese soft power in Europe" (Duchâtel, 2015). The audit targeted government officials and experts of Japan in academia, media, and think tanks and aimed to study the image of Japan as a partner in nine European countries – Austria, France, Germany, Italy, Poland, Portugal, Spain, Sweden, and the United Kingdom. Rethinking and enhancing Japan's public diplomacy strategies is essential for achieving a higher cultural presence in Europe.

A crucial reason for the insufficient Japanese soft power in Europe has been the lack of integration among the public diplomacy actors and their initiatives. Most of the public and private actors promoting Japanese culture have been acting autonomously, without having a particular central actor to unify and facilitate their projects as well as without a common strategy. As Watanabe (2012) highlights, for a more productive public diplomacy, Japan needs "organic integration of organizations and projects". A major actor facilitating partnerships for cooperation between Japan's public and private institutions for cultural promotion in Europe is essential.

To provide such an integrated approach, Japan has emphasized the Cool Japan Public-Private Partnership initiative of the Cabinet Office. However, the initiative is focused mainly on promoting the Cool Japan Strategy and on strengthening collaborations among the industries in the Cool Japan fields. In addition, Cool Japan reaches out mostly to the younger generations rather than to the elite, middle-aged, or senior generations. Therefore, it is vital for Japan to work on a new approach facilitated by a Japanese public diplomacy actor with a wide network of partners, which would coordinate public-private cooperation among institutions and actors from all kind of fields and Japanese cultural spheres as well as reach a variety of generations at the same time.

In response to the above-mentioned issue, this study examines the potential of the Japan Foundation as a central public diplomacy actor in Europe, facilitating a Public-Private Partnership[1] Platform for integrated initiatives among actors and institutions in charge of Japanese cultural promotion. Since its establishment in 1972, the Foundation has been playing a significant role in the dissemination of Japanese culture abroad. It has specific contributions and advantages as well. For instance, in comparison with other Japanese institutions, the Japan Foundation has the broadest network of public and private partners for cultural promotion worldwide. It works both autonomously and together with crucial actors and provides funds to individuals and organizations for the conduct of cultural projects. Considering the challenges in the financial system of Japan, spending money on multiple actors of public diplomacy may not be cost efficient. Therefore, if Japan maximizes the potential of the Japan Foundation, it would economize funds and maintain collaboration with many actors at the same time. An essential feature of the Japan Foundation is also the broad type of audience that it reaches, ranging from the younger generation to the elite, the middle-aged, and the senior generation. Another advantage of the Japan Foundation is its crucial role in the nurturing of a long-term interest towards Japanese culture abroad. Despite the current popularity of Japan worldwide, according to Watanabe (2018), "as time passes, foreign culture comes to seem ordinary and people tire of it" and "the vogue for Japan will one day reach its sell-by date". In order to maintain a continuous interest towards Japan, it is essential to establish new cultural values and reconsider the direction of its cultural promotion policies. Japan should work to introduce its daily life and customs, philosophies, and attitudes towards life and nature and the history and origin of Japanese arts and products. In facing this challenge, the Japan Foundation is highly contributory. First, through its cultural projects abroad, the Foundation has been working to present a variety of Japanese values and cultural aspects. Second, it promotes the Japanese language, which "helps foster future leaders who will build a bridge between Japan and overseas, deepen understanding towards Japan, and lay a foundation for friendship with other countries" (Ministry of Foreign Affairs of Japan, 2017). Third, the Japan Foundation implements Japanese studies and intellectual exchange programs providing opportunities for two-way exchanges between Japan and the world. The participants are able to visit Japan, experience its culture, and develop new relationships. Through all these initiatives, the Foundation contributes to maintaining and further deepening foreign people's long-term interest in Japan.

Some of the advantages and features of the Japan Foundation are its considerable capacity and prospects for coordinating and implementing integrated Japanese public diplomacy initiatives in Europe. By facilitating a Public-Private Partnership Platform, the Foundation could strengthen the collaborations between the public and private sectors, reach out to various generations, create a stable basis for Japan's further relations with Europe, and compensate for the scarceness of soft power on the continent.

The purpose of this study is to analyze an integrated approach for Japanese public diplomacy in Europe through public-private partnerships. The study's aim is also to examine the potential and limitations of the Japan Foundation as a major public diplomacy actor in charge of such a Public-Private Partnership Platform as well as to suggest a framework of recommendations concerning its future initiatives in Europe both autonomously and in collaboration with other institutions.

The observations and discussions in the study focus on two European countries: France – a country where the Japan Foundation's office has been established, and Bulgaria – where an office of the Japan Foundation does not exist, but the Japanese Embassy has been facilitating programs of the Foundation. In order to provide a more profound analysis and recommendations for Japan's further public diplomacy initiatives on the continent, it is essential to compare and examine Japan's cultural promotion in countries from both Western and Eastern[2] Europe, especially those that differ in terms of the existence of the Foundation's office. Such countries are France and Bulgaria, where the Japan Foundation has been playing a great role in the introduction of various aspects of Japanese culture as well as in the creation of a positive image of the country.

The reason for focusing on France as a case study from Western Europe is the fact that Japanese culture has been promoted to a greater extent there than in other countries on the continent. As Masuda (Lavallée, 2018), emphasizes, France is more familiar with Japan than any other nation in Europe. In addition, as a former ambassador of France to Japan highlighted during his personal communication with the author of this study, "among European countries, France is certainly, culturally speaking, the most appreciated country open to Japanese cultural impact and keen to get it" (personal communication, May 12, 2019). An example of Japan's great cultural promotion activity in France has been the Japonismes 2018 event, held in commemoration of the 160th anniversary of the diplomatic relations between the two countries. According to Japan's Prime Minister Shinzo Abe, the Japonismes 2018 initiative has been "Japan's largest endeavor to share Japanese culture with the world" (Japonismes 2018, 2018).

There are three specific reasons for focusing on Bulgaria as a case study from Eastern Europe.

The first is Bulgaria's strong and active bilateral cultural relations with Japan, which have provided and continue to provide a favorable atmosphere for Japanese cultural promotion. Bulgaria is the first Eastern European country to fall under Ottoman rule, which lasted for almost five centuries (1396–1878). There is evidence that the Japanese officer Yamazawa Seigo participated in the Russo-Turkish War for the liberation of Bulgaria in 1878 (Embassy of Japan in Bulgaria, n.d.-b). The country proclaimed its independence in 1908. Despite its dramatic history and considerably slower recovery, Bulgaria has managed to develop its cultural relationship with Japan. From the 1900s on, bilateral interactions increased, especially with the Friendship and Cultural Cooperation Agreement between the governments of Bulgaria and Japan, signed in February 1943 in Tokyo. For instance, even though it became invalid when diplomatic relations were interrupted from 1944 to 1959, as a result of the impact of the World War

II, the countries maintained their intercultural interactions. In addition, in the Cold War period until its transition to a multiparty democracy and a functioning market economy in 1989, Bulgaria, as a socialist country, was not much open to cultural promotion from any capitalistic country. Despite these limitations, Bulgarian-Japanese intercultural activities continued in a broad perspective. At the time, Japanese public diplomacy played a crucial role in developing Bulgarian people's interest in and positive image of Japan. Such an example is the 1970 World Exposition in Japan, considered a highly contributory event to the further progress of the cultural, economic, and political bilateral relations. Attended by the Bulgarian Prime Minister Todor Zhivkov, the Expo'70 exhibition made Bulgaria aware of the so-called Japanese economic miracle and its coexistence with tradition and harmony with nature as well as various aspects of Japanese culture. The event is thought to have increased the country's interest in economic and technical collaboration with Japan. In 1975, a new agreement on cooperation in science, art, and culture between the governments of Bulgaria and Japan was signed, under which various bilateral cultural initiatives have been implemented. At the same time, public diplomacy has been accompanied by high-level bilateral dialogue on a state and governmental level.

Another example of the deep bilateral cultural ties is the fact that Bulgaria has been visited by various members of the Japanese Imperial Family. In 1979, it was visited by the Japanese Crown Prince Akihito and Crown Princess Michiko as official representatives of Emperor Hirohito. The visit was a significant event symbolizing the warm and friendly relations between the two countries. In the following years, Bulgaria was visited by Their Highnesses Prince and Princess Mikasa in 1987, Her Highness Princess Sayako in 1996, and Their Highnesses Prince and Princess Akishino in 2009. After their visits, the members of the Japanese Imperial Family have expressed a high interest in the Bulgarian cultural initiatives held in Japan by personally attending some of the events.

As a member of the European Union since 2007, Bulgarian cultural relations with Japan continued to develop in new dimensions. There have been various examples like the Bulgarian Sumo wrestler Kaloyan Mahlyanov (Kotooshu), who was made the Goodwill Ambassador to Japan by the European Union in 2006. This event demonstrated the recognition that Kotooshu was present in the Japanese Sumo sport not only as a Bulgarian, but also as a European representative, and the cultural relations between Bulgaria and Japan were commensurate with that between Europe and Japan (Vutova-Stefanova, 2016, p. 164). Bulgaria has also been participating in a number of joint European cultural and educational initiatives in Japan, organized by the embassies of the European Union member countries and the Delegation of the European Union to Japan. "The Golden Legend" exhibition organized in 2016 in Japan, consisting of 280 exhibits from nine European countries including Bulgaria's ancient Thracian treasures, is a case in point.

The second reason for focusing on Bulgaria is the fact that there is much potential and a favorable atmosphere for Japanese public diplomacy, especially through public-private partnerships between the Japan Foundation and Bulgarian institutions. For instance, since the establishment of the Japanese language and studies major at the Sofia University "St. Kliment Ohridski", in cooperation with the Japan Foundation the university has been organizing a variety of Japanese language and culture promotion projects with the aim of becoming a center for the study of Japanese language and culture on the Balkans (Koleva, 2016, p. 245). One such initiative, held annually since 2012, is the Balkan Peninsula Japanese language and culture summer camp in Bulgaria, in which countries like Romania, Turkey, North Macedonia, and Serbia take part. Although there is still space for further improvement of these projects, they have been acknowledged by the Japanese language teaching community in Eastern Europe (Koleva, 2016, pp. 246–247).

The third reason is the fact that Bulgaria is a country demonstrating a strong interest in Japanese culture, but with limited opportunities for experiencing it, which provides much space for further Japanese cultural promotion initiatives (Embassy of Japan in Bulgaria, n.d.-a). Exploring the insufficient points and the future possibilities for enhancing and expanding Japan's cultural activities in Bulgaria is crucial. In addition, the results from the study on Bulgaria could serve as a basis for any future comparative research of Japan's public diplomacy in Eastern Europe.

Together with the reasons emphasized earlier, the author's Bulgarian language ability, and contacts within the country, providing opportunities for a greater accessibility to a broad range of sources as well as to various experts and figures for the conduct of interviews is also essential. This enables the author to implement a more in-depth study of Japan's public diplomacy in Bulgaria in comparison with such examination in other countries in Eastern Europe.

Starting with an introduction, the study is divided into five sections. It begins with a focus on the basic concept – public diplomacy. Certain definitions and subsets of public diplomacy, as well as its differences with traditional diplomacy, are emphasized. The next section explores Japan's public diplomacy from the 1860s to present. It highlights the main Japanese public diplomacy actors, including the Ministry of Foreign Affairs and the Japan Foundation as well as other essential institutions like the Cabinet Office and its Cool Japan Strategy. The next section investigates the Japanese cultural promotion in France and Bulgaria with a special focus on the Japan Foundation and its initiatives between the 1970s and 2018 in the following three categories: art and cultural exchange, Japanese-language education, and Japanese studies and intellectual exchange. The study examines the Foundation's contributions and activities implemented both autonomously and in collaboration with Japanese and local public and private actors in the two countries. It also compares the Foundation's initiatives in France and Bulgaria, highlighting both the strong and the insufficient points in terms of its cultural promotion. Based on the findings, it provides a framework of suggestions concerning the Foundation's future projects in the areas. The next section of the study discusses the potential and limitations of the Japan Foundation for becoming Japan's central public diplomacy actor facilitating a Public-Private Partnership Platform in Europe. Following this, the study explores essential Japanese and local public and private actors who have the potential for future cooperation with the Japan Foundation through such partnerships. It discusses specific benefits for Japan's future public diplomacy resulting from the establishment of this Public-Private Partnership Platform. Finally, through personal interviews of the author with Bulgarian and French representatives, the study examines the image of Japan and the future expectations from Japan in the two countries. Understanding local perceptions is vital for improving and building on current policies. Based on the feedback, it reveals certain cultural aspects, elements, and insufficient and less explored areas of Japanese soft power, which could be further introduced for increasing the Japanese presence in those areas. In response to these findings, the study suggests specific project proposals for integrated public diplomacy initiatives in France and Bulgaria through the Public-Private Partnership Platform facilitated by the Japan Foundation.

The research method applied in this study is qualitative. To observe the concept of public diplomacy, Japan's public diplomacy actors and initiatives, as well as Japanese cultural promotion in France and Bulgaria, various Bulgarian, English, French and Japanese academic sources were reviewed. Due to the lack of any published sources on the topic, the discussion on the Japan Foundation's initiatives in France and Bulgaria was constructed based on the full lists of activities implemented between 1973 and 2018 in those two countries. The lists are unpublished documents, kindly provided to the author of the present study by the Foundation. They consist of 676 projects in Bulgaria and 4618 in France, which were classified in three categories and translated from Japanese into English for this study. The originality of this study makes it a good reference for any future research in this field. In addition, to examine the image of Japan and the future expectations from Japan in France and Bulgaria, personal interviews with Bulgarian and French representatives were conducted by the author. The interviews were qualitative, aimed at collecting personal opinion from experts and individuals with considerable experience, familiarity, and interest in Japanese culture. This included Bulgarian and French government officials, scholars, and representatives of the young and middle-aged generations.

Notes

1 There is not a single, agreed-upon definition of Public-Private Partnership. For example, according to the European Regional Development Fund (2017, p. 6), it could be described as a "form of cooperation between public and private sector" as well as an "undertaking that brings benefits to both involved parties proportionally to their involvement". In this study, Public-Private Partnership will be considered a form of cooperation between the public and private sector on the planning and implementation of certain projects.
2 In this study, the concept of Eastern Europe does not include Central European countries such as Austria, Czech Republic, Croatia, Hungary, Poland, Slovakia, and Slovenia.

References

Duchâtel, M. (2015, December 7). The new Japan paradox. *European Council on Foreign Relations*. Retrieved August 20, 2018, from www.ecfr.eu/article/ commentary_the_new_japan_paradox5044

Embassy of Japan in Bulgaria. (n.d.-a). Kulturen Obmen [Cultural exchange]. *Dvustranni otnosheniya* [Bilateral relations]. Retrieved December 28, 2019, from www.bg.emb-japan.go.jp/bg/bg_jap_relations/culture_exchange/index.html

Embassy of Japan in Bulgaria. (n.d.-b). *Reisen shūryō-ji made no Burugaria to Nihon no gaikō* [Bulgarian-Japanese relations until the end of the cold war]. Retrieved November 16, 2020, from www.bg.emb-japan.go.jp/jp/downloads/ nihontomonokai_lecture_ivanov.pdf

European Regional Development Fund. (2017). Handbook on public-private partnership (PPP) in built heritage revitalisation projects. *RESTAURA. Interreg Central Europe*. Retrieved from www.interreg-central.eu/Content.Node/O. T1.1-Handbook-new.pdf

Japonismes 2018. (2018). *Japonismes 2018: les âmes en resonance* [Japonismes 2018: Souls in resonance]. Retrieved from https://japonismes.org/en/about#background

Koleva, E. (2016). Novi metodi v prepodavaneto na yaponski ezik [New teaching methods of Japanese language]. In P. Gergana, A. Andreev, E. Koleva, & A. Todorova (Eds.), *Japan – Times, spirituality and perspectives* (pp. 238–247). Sofia: Universitetsko izdatelstvo "Sv. Kliment Ohridski".

Lavallée, G. (2018, July 15). France goes big on Japan with multi-million cultural program. *Rappler*. Retrieved from www.rappler.com/world/regions/ europe/207213-france-japan-multi-million-cultural-program

Ministry of Foreign Affairs of Japan. (2017). *Diplomatic Bluebook 2017: Japan's foreign policy to promote national and worldwide interests*. Retrieved from www. mofa.go.jp/policy/other/bluebook/2017/html/chapter3/c030402.html

Ogawa, T. (2009). Origin and development of Japan's public diplomacy. In N. Snow & P. M. Taylor (Eds.), *Routledge handbook of public diplomacy* (pp. 270–281). New York, NY and London: Routledge.

Vutova-Stefanova, V. (2016). Bulariya-Yaponiya, Dialog i obmen mejdu dve kulturi [Bulgaria-Japan, dialogue and exchange between two cultures]. In P. Gergana, A. Andreev, E. Koleva, & A. Todorova (Eds.), *Japan – Times, spirituality and perspectives* (pp. 137–169). Sofia: Universitetsko izdatelstvo "Sv. Kliment Ohridski".

Watanabe, H. (2012, April 20). Japan's cultural diplomacy future. *The Diplomat.* Retrieved from https://thediplomat.com/2012/04/japans-cultural-diplomacy-future/

Watanabe, H. (2018). The new Japonisme: From international cultural exchange to cultural diplomacy – Evaluating the influence of cultural activities on diplomacy. *Discuss Japan, Japan Foreign Policy Forum, Ministry of Foreign Affairs of Japan. Diplomacy*, 50. Retrieved from www.japanpolicyforum.jp/diplomacy/pt201810301300038356.html

2 The concept of "public diplomacy"

Soft power and public diplomacy

Public diplomacy is closely linked to power. In the international society, it has been regarded as a vital instrument for wielding soft power. According to Nye (2004, p. 2), power might be defined as "the ability to influence the behavior of others to get the outcomes one wants". There could be different ways to affect the behavior of others – through the use of force, payment, and threats typical to "hard power" or by attraction and persuasion characteristic of "soft power".

The term "soft power" was first coined by Harvard University professor Joseph Nye. He defined it as "the ability to affect others through the co-optive means of framing the agenda, persuading, and eliciting positive attraction in order to obtain preferred outcomes" (Nye, 2011, p. 21). Through the practice of soft power, the aims of a particular country could be achieved "because other countries – admiring its values, emulating its example, aspiring to its level of prosperity and openness – want to follow it" (Nye, 2004, p. 5). In addition, soft power is interpreted as the use of culture as a form of diplomatic policy, also identified as public diplomacy or cultural diplomacy. It characterizes the connection between a country's cultural initiatives and diplomacy abroad.

In the digital age, international society and the nature of power have changed, and the importance of soft power and public diplomacy has been rising. Communication strategies have become more essential and "outcomes are shaped not merely by whose army wins but also by whose story wins" (Nye, 2011, p. 19). Public diplomacy has become a crucial instrument for expanding a country's cultural presence and creating a basis for prosperous and harmonious relations between states.

Definitions and subsets of "public diplomacy"

The basic mechanism for implementing a country's foreign politics is diplomacy. In the past, mostly common among governments was classical

DOI: 10.4324/9781003006251-2

diplomacy, also called "cabinet diplomacy", which consisted of sending messages between rulers, usually in confidential communications. Besides this direct type of communication, governments discovered an indirect route, which gave them the opportunity to communicate with the publics of other countries in an effort to influence other governments. This indirect form of diplomacy was recognized as public diplomacy (Nye, 2011, pp. 101–102).

The term "public diplomacy" was coined for the first time in 1965 by Edmund Gullion, dean of the Fletcher School of Law and Diplomacy at Tufts University and founder of the Edward R. Murrow Center of Public Diplomacy. One of the early brochures of the Murrow Center published a summary of Gullion's definition of the notion of public diplomacy indicating:

> Public diplomacy . . . deals with the influence of public attitudes on the formation and execution of foreign policies. It encompasses dimensions of international relations beyond traditional diplomacy; the cultivation by governments of public opinion in other countries; the interaction of private groups and interests in one country with another; the reporting of foreign affairs and its impact on policy; communication between those whose job is communication, as diplomats and foreign correspondents; and the process of intercultural communications.
>
> (Cull, 2009a, p. 19)

Another definition of public diplomacy is provided by Paul Sharp, who recognizes it as "the process by which direct relations with people in a country are pursued to advance the interests and extend the values of those being represented" (Melissen, 2005b, p. 8). Here, the emphasis is on ordinary people, and the response from the public is considered important for deciding further steps for the achievement of desired outcomes.

According to the USC Center on Public Diplomacy (n.d.), public diplomacy could be interpreted as "the public, interactive dimension of diplomacy which is not only global in nature, but also involves a multitude of actors and networks", and it is "a key mechanism through which nations foster mutual trust and productive relationships and has become crucial to building a secure global environment". In other words, a wide range of actors and networks are involved in public diplomacy, and their role in nurturing prosperous and harmonious relations between countries is of utmost importance.

As demonstrated previously, different descriptions of public diplomacy are given by practitioners, academics, research institutes, and governments, and there is no single agreed-upon definition. While the rich palette of definitions provides the opportunity to explore public diplomacy from various perspectives, it might also lead to some difficulties in fully understanding the concept. For instance, certain skeptics interpret the term "public diplomacy" as a synonym for propaganda. As Welch (Melissen, 2005b, p. 20) describes it, propaganda is "the deliberate attempts to influence the opinions of an audience through the transmission of ideas and values for the specific purpose, consciously designed to serve the interests of the propagandists and their political masters, either directly or indirectly". Such definitions could cause confusion or difficulties in noticing the difference between public diplomacy and propaganda. However, it is vital to distinguish between the two notions. They differ in terms of the pattern of communication. According to Melissen (2005b, p. 22), "public diplomacy is similar to propaganda in that it tries to persuade people what to think, but it is fundamentally different from it in the sense that public diplomacy also listens to what people have to say". In addition, as McClellan (2004) highlights, when propaganda is applied, "a particular message is 'injected' into the target country over and over", while public diplomacy is based on "the active, planned use of cultural, educational and informational programming to effect a desired result that is directly related to a government's foreign policy objectives".

Public diplomacy consists of specific subsets through which it has been implemented. Such include cultural diplomacy, listening, advocacy, international broadcasting, and exchanges (Cull, 2009b, p. 10). Although the terms public diplomacy and cultural diplomacy might look similar, as they are both elements of the soft power, they should not be equated. Cultural diplomacy, as Leonard (Mark, 2009, p. 6) describes it, is "that part of public diplomacy that is concerned with the building of long-term relationships". According to the U.S. Advisory Commission on Public Diplomacy (2005, p. 4), cultural diplomacy is "the linchpin of public diplomacy; for it is in cultural activities that a nation's idea of itself is best represented". In addition, public diplomacy and cultural diplomacy differ in terms of their objectives and the scope of their activities. Public diplomacy consists of a wider set of activities than does cultural diplomacy, "primarily those government media and public relations activities aimed at a foreign public in order to explain a course of action, or present a case" (Mark, 2009, p. 15). According to Ogoura (2009, p. 45), the difference between public diplomacy and cultural diplomacy is that "the former is always closely associated with a well-defined political objective and aimed at certain pre-determined targets while the latter is not necessarily linked to a specific political objective".

Differences between public diplomacy and traditional diplomacy

The traditional understanding of diplomatic practice has been mostly associated with ideas like "elitism, strict confidentiality, expertise, lofty professionalism and, last but not least, meticulous diplomatic protocol involving representative functions" (Simova & Katrandjiev, 2014, p. 134). The vast recent changes in the international society and the increasing impact of globalization require a novel approach to understanding diplomacy as well as modifications in the methods of communication and the actors involved in it. According to Genov (2014, p. 2), the new understanding of diplomacy considers the notion as a "business, which does not involve only foreign ministries, their diplomats, embassies and consulates". Genov (2014, p. 2) also points out,

> traditional diplomacy has adapted to the changes in the society such as the higher level of democratization, empowerment of the society and greater attention to morality and values. In this way diplomacy now focuses on the public expectations and preferences, human rights, cultural differences, international law, transparency and accountability.

This makes diplomacy a suitable and preferred tool in the international relations between countries. The opening of the diplomatic offices to "the needs of civil society and turning these offices into a function of social and political relations in the broadest sense of the world" leads to a new public attitude towards the diplomatic profession and practice (Simova & Katrandjiev, 2014, p. 134).

It is important to distinguish public diplomacy from traditional diplomacy. There have been various definitions by scholars, who highlight the difference between these two concepts. For example, as Edward Murrow mentioned in his speech in 1963 (Leonard et al., 2002, p. 1), "public diplomacy differs from traditional diplomacy not only with governments but primarily with non-governmental individuals and organizations". According to Cull (2009b, p. 12), traditional diplomacy is an "international actor's attempt to manage the international environment through engagement with another international actor", while public diplomacy is "an international actor's attempts to manage the international environment through engagement with a foreign public". Figure 2.1 introduces certain differences between public and traditional diplomacy.

Public Diplomacy	Traditional Diplomacy
❖ Indirect diplomacy	❖ Direct diplomacy
❖ Unofficial diplomacy	❖ Official diplomacy
❖ Engagement with the public	❖ Confidential
❖ Mutuality and focus on foreign public expectations	❖ Comprehension
❖ Exchange with the public	❖ One-way informational diplomacy

Figure 2.1 Public Diplomacy vs. Traditional Diplomacy

The new public diplomacy

Recently, scholars have emphasized the so-called *new* public diplomacy, which indicates some shifts in the practice of public diplomacy. According to Melissen (2005a, p. 22), the new public diplomacy is "no longer confined to messaging, promotion campaigns, or even direct governmental contacts with foreign publics serving foreign policy purposes"; it is also about "building relationships with civil society actors in other countries and about facilitating networks between non-governmental parties at home and abroad". In addition, the new public diplomacy overlaps in certain aspects with cultural relations. As Melissen (2005a, pp. 21–22) highlights,

> in cultural relations as much as in the new public diplomacy, the accent is increasingly on engaging with foreign audiences rather than selling messages, on mutuality and the establishment of stable relationships instead of mere policy-driven campaigns, on the "long haul" rather than short-term needs, and on winning "hearts and minds" and building trust.

There are specific differences between the old and the new public diplomacy practices. According to Cull (2009b, pp. 12–13), the new public diplomacy consists of the following characteristics:

> 1) the international actors are increasingly non-traditional and NGOs are especially prominent; 2) the mechanisms used by these actors to communicate with world publics have moved into new, real-time and global technologies (especially the Internet); 3) these new technologies have blurred the formerly rigid lines between the domestic and

international news spheres; 4) in place of old concepts of propaganda Public Diplomacy makes increasing use of concepts on one hand explicitly derived from marketing – especially place and nation branding – and on the other hand concepts growing from network communication theory; hence, there is 5) a new terminology of Public Diplomacy as the language of prestige and international image has given way to talk of "soft power" and "branding".

In addition, while the old public diplomacy focuses on the actor-to-people communication model, typical to the new public diplomacy is the people-to-people contact for mutual enlightenment, in which the international actor is the main facilitator.

For the conduct of an effective new public diplomacy, government policy should participate in networks abroad, rather than controlling them. If governments exercise too much control, the credibility established by the networks might be damaged. As Nye (2011, p. 108) emphasizes,

> for governments to succeed in the networked world of the new public diplomacy, they are going to have to learn to relinquish a good deal of their control, and this runs the risk that nongovernmental civil society actors are often not aligned in their goals with government policies or even objectives.

References

Cull, N. J. (2009a). Public diplomacy before gullion: The evolution of a phase. In N. Snow & P. M. Taylor (Eds.), *Routledge handbook of public diplomacy* (pp. 19–23). New York, NY and London: Routledge.

Cull, N. J. (2009b). *Public diplomacy: Lessons from the past*. Los Angeles, CA: Figueroa Press.

Genov, G. (2014). *Diplomatsiyata na XXI vek* [The diplomacy of XXI century]. Sofia: Balkan Analytica.

Leonard, M., Stead, C., & Smewing, C. (2002). *Public diplomacy*. London: The Foreign Policy Centre.

Mark, S. (2009). *A greater role for cultural diplomacy* (Discussion papers in diplomacy). The Hague: Netherlands Institute of International Relations 'Clingendael'.

McClellan, M. (2004, October 14). *Public diplomacy in the context of traditional diplomacy*. Retrieved from www.publicdiplomacy.org/45.htm

Melissen, J. (2005a). The new public diplomacy: Between theory and practice. In J. Melissen (Ed.), *The new public diplomacy: Soft power in international relations* (pp. 3–27). London: Palgrave Macmillan.

Melissen, J. (2005b). *Wielding soft power: The new public diplomacy* (Clingendael Diplomacy Papers No. 2). The Hague: Netherlands Institute of International Relations Clingendael.

Nye, J., Jr. (2004). *Soft power: The means to success in world politics.* New York, NY: PublicAffairs.

Nye, J., Jr. (2011). *The future of power.* New York, NY: PublicAffairs.

Ogoura, K. (2009). *Japan's cultural diplomacy, past and present.* Tokyo: Joint Research Institute for International Peace and Culture, Aoyama Gakuin University, pp. 44–54.

Simova, N., & Katrandjiev, V. (2014). *The inter-professional dimension of modern diplomacy.* Sofia: Diplomatic Institute, Ministry of Foreign Affairs Republic of Bulgaria, pp. 134–146.

U.S. Advisory Commission on Public Diplomacy. (2005). *Cultural diplomacy: The linchpin of public diplomacy* (Report of the Advisory Committee on Cultural Diplomacy). Washington, DC: U.S. Department of State.

USC Center on Public Diplomacy. (n.d.). *What is public diplomacy?* Retrieved August 20, 2021, from http://uscpublicdiplomacy.org/page/what-pdf

3 Japan's public diplomacy

Public diplomacy initiatives before World War II

As Ogawa (2009, p. 272) emphasizes, some of Japan's first public diplomacy activities can be recognized in the 1860s, when the country began its process of modernization. Some examples include its participation in World Expositions like the second International Exhibition of 1862 in London, the second International Exposition of 1867 in Paris, and others,[1] as well as certain public relations activities implemented during the Russo-Japanese War. In addition, the establishment of Rokumeikan in 1883 in Tokyo for welcoming foreign guests and holding Westernized balls is also a case in point. Meanwhile, Japan's goal was the revising of the "unequal treaties"[2] that it had signed with the United States and European great powers. Therefore, it "needed to promote itself both at home and overseas not as a colony of the great powers, but as a modernized nation with a proper culture, and as worthy of forming an equal relationship with the United States and the European great powers" (Watanabe, 2018).

At the time, Japan's most-used public diplomacy instrument was the media. As Watanabe (2018) highlights, the government "made allies of journalists and influential people and had them write pro-Japanese articles in English newspapers and other publications" in Europe and the United States. In this way, Japanese cultural diplomacy and politics went hand in hand.

After World War I, Japan strengthened its commitment to external public relations and cultural diplomacy. In 1920, the Ministry of Foreign Affairs of Japan (MOFA) created the Department of Information and also began new programs for cultural exchange with China. These programs aimed to mitigate the anti-Japanese sentiment that from the 1910s was growing among Chinese intellectuals (Ogawa, 2009, p. 273).

In the 1920s and the 1930s, various structures for public diplomacy were founded in the West. These included cultural exchange organizations

DOI: 10.4324/9781003006251-3

like Germany's Goethe Institute in 1932 and the United Kingdom's British Council in 1934. At the same time, in 1934, Japan "became the first and only non-Western nation to establish a modern international cultural exchange organization" (Ogawa, 2009, p. 273). The Society for International Cultural Relations (Kokusai Bunka Shinko-kai, or KBS) was created through certain financial support from the government and the private sector. One of the reasons for the establishment of KBS could be considered Japan's diplomatic isolation in the 1930s after it walked out of the League of Nations (Ogawa, 2009, p. 273).

KBS carried out a variety of initiatives such as "dialogues among prominent cultural leaders, dispatch of cultural missions, and publications on Japan" (Ogawa, 2009, p. 273). In the 1930s, its main focus was on the United States and Europe. However, when World War II started, KBS aimed to "win the hearts and minds" of the local residents in the places under Japanese occupation (Ogawa, 2009, p. 273). Following this, the organization's priority became China and Southeast Asia.

Public diplomacy initiatives after World War II

After World War II, Japan's external public relations and cultural exchange activities were interrupted. In December 1945, the Cabinet Bureau of Information stopped functioning. Although the Department of Information was reestablished by MOFA in 1946, it lacked enough budget and staff to conduct its prewar cultural exchange initiatives.

In the 1950s and the early 1960s, Japan began to exercise cultural diplomacy, a subset of its public diplomacy, with the aim of altering the "prewar image of Japan as a militaristic country into a new image of Japan as a peace-loving democracy" (Ogoura, 2009, p. 46). As Ogawa (2009, p. 274) points out, Prime Minister Tetsu Katayama highlighted in a policy speech that it was necessary for Japan to construct a "culture state in order to restore national pride and international credibility". According to Kaneko (2007, p. 187), the Japanese government developed a new strategy that centered on the establishment and promotion of a harmonious and cultural image of the country. In 1951, Japan joined UNESCO to restore its status in international organizations. For Japan, the process of creating a peace-loving and democratic state was closely linked to the dissemination of cultural activities, which provided the country with a new national identity (Ogoura, 2009, p. 46).

The introduction of Japanese culture abroad included practices like tea ceremony and ikebana, as they would demonstrate Japan's serene and peaceful nature to the world. In addition, most of the pamphlets and brochures on Japan available at the time consisted of cherry blossoms and Mount Fuji pictures, symbolizing tranquility and serenity (Ogoura, 2009, p. 46). On the other hand, elements of Japanese culture connected to samurai spirit or feudal traditions were not promoted.

In the 1960s, Japan reached a high level of economic development. The new objective of its cultural diplomacy was to project an image of a technologically and economically advanced nation. Examples of such initiatives include the hosting of the Tokyo Olympics in 1964 and the 1970 Expo in Osaka. In addition, with the creation of the Economic Cooperation Bureau and its membership in the Organisation for Economic Co-operation and Development (OECD), Japan's status in the international community was growing. In 1968, the Agency for Cultural Affairs was founded as well (Ogawa, 2009, p. 274). Japan enhanced its overseas cultural activities by establishing cultural and information centers attached to embassies, establishing the Japanese Language Society for Foreigners in 1962, and accomplishing certain cultural exchange agreements with socialist countries between 1969 and 1979 (Ogoura, 2009, p. 47).

At the same time, Japan's economic growth led to certain anti-Japanese sentiments and misunderstandings about Japanese culture around the world. It became vital for the Japanese government to build up its public diplomacy strategies. As Ogawa (2009, p. 275) highlights, "suffering from a series of Japan-U.S. frictions over trade imbalances and the Nixon Shocks, the Japanese diplomatic community began to recognize combating misunderstanding about Japanese culture and behavior as an urgent diplomatic agenda". As a result, in 1972, there was a major step in the history of Japanese public diplomacy. The Japan Foundation – a large organization for cultural exchange – was established. Supervised under the Cultural Division of MOFA, the Foundation began a variety of programs such as "exchange among prominent academic and cultural leaders, promotion of Japanese language education and Japanese studies overseas, concerts, exhibitions, Japanese film and television showings, and publications" (Ogawa, 2009, p. 275).

In the late 1980s, with the development of its economy, Japan occupied a greater position in the international society. The country was expected to "make more contributions as a responsible partner in the international community", and thus its cultural diplomacy began to be considered "one of the 'three pillars' of Japan's foreign policy – the first being the country's contributions to peacekeeping operations or similar activities and the second being its official developmental assistance or economic aid policies" (Ogoura, 2009, p. 48).

At the time, there has been demand from various countries worldwide for Japan to become more "internationalized" by "opening up culturally and intellectually to the international community" (Ogoura, 2009,

p. 49). Following this, in 1984 the Department of Cultural Exchange was created by MOFA. In addition, in 1987 the JET program began to exist, thanks to which many foreign language teachers and international exchange coordinators are being invited to Japan every year. According to Ogawa (2009, p. 276), its objectives were "internationalizing Japan's local communities by helping to improve foreign language education" as well as establishing "grassroots channels between Japan and the rest of the world" and developing "the next generation of supporters of Japan".

In the 1980s, for the first time in Japan's diplomatic history, cultural exchange was considered a main priority for the country (Ogawa, 2009, p. 276). In 1988, a report by the Advisory Group on International Cultural Exchange indicated a high necessity for Japan to strengthen its international cultural exchange, as well as suggested certain policies such as the enhancing of the budgets for the Japan Foundation and direct support from the government. Consequently, the government increased its funding to the Japan Foundation, and the Conference for the Promotion of International Cultural Exchange was founded in 1989. MOFA also created a new post of press secretary, which unified and coordinated the controls in public relations.

In the mid-1990s, Japan's public diplomacy acquired a new dimension. Recognized as a responsible partner in the community of the developed nations, Japan had to redefine its own cultural identity and to show an image of itself "not as a newcomer to the developed nation's club but as a truly responsible and mature partner" (Ogoura, 2009, p. 50). Therefore, the country began to emphasize the promotion of postmodern culture such as anime, *manga*, fashion, pop music, and other contemporary trends. These activities also linked Japan's public diplomacy to its trade policy. In addition, the combination of Japanese electronic technology with traditional culture was gaining popularity as well.

In recent years, Japan is not the only highly economically developed country in Asia. Therefore, in order to distinguish itself from China, South Korea, and other Asian countries, Japan transformed the dimension of its cultural diplomacy by centering on "a hybrid vision of Japan, a combination of the old and the new" (Ogoura, 2009, p. 50). This tendency of mixing the old and the new can be illustrated by the Great Edo Exhibition, which opened in London in 1995.

In August 2004, the Public Diplomacy Department was created due to a structural reform that divided the labor between MOFA and the Japan Foundation. Since then, the department has a variety of functions such as "implementing international agreements to promote cultural exchange, cooperating with international cultural organizations, and introducing Japanese culture abroad and promoting cultural exchange with foreign countries" (Ogawa, 2009, p. 278).

In December 2004, the Council on the Promotion of Cultural Diplomacy was launched by Japanese Prime Minister Junichiro Koizumi. The council emphasized, "understanding Japan by the public of a country may be the most influential factor for the government of that country in deciding policies and actions toward Japan" (Ogawa, 2009, p. 278). It also made some suggestions on the challenges and tactics of Japanese cultural diplomacy. The council highlighted, "Japan should try to actively cultivate a 'Japanese animation generation' across the globe, seizing interest in the Japanese language and pop culture as an opportunity to encourage further interest in other aspects of diverse Japanese culture" (Ogawa, 2009, pp. 278–279).

In 2005, following a report from the Council on the Promotion of Cultural Diplomacy, the Japanese government started to put a great emphasis on Japan's soft power exercised through cultural diplomacy. The report suggested a policy according to which "diverse aspects of Japanese culture, both traditional and modern, would be communicated to the world" (Watanabe, 2018). Since 2010, Japanese cultural activities abroad became systematically prioritized (Watanabe, 2018). In 2013, the MOFA Advisory Council on Public Diplomacy conducted various meetings regarding Japanese public diplomacy initiatives. As a result, a variety of projects introducing Japanese culture overseas were implemented. Such examples are the Japan Houses established in San Paulo (2017), Los Angeles (2017), and London (2018).

In 2009, another initiative aimed at increasing Japanese soft power abroad was the Japan Brand Strategy, released by the "Contents and Japan Brand Specialist Research Group" of the Cabinet Office Intellectual Property Strategy Headquarters. The strategy "identified anime, game contents, food, fashion" and other trends as "soft power industries" and "clarified their strategic representation and communication as 'Japan Brand' (strengthening creativity, strengthening the ability to disseminate information, and building structures)" (Watanabe, 2018).

At present, within the globalized international society, Japanese cultural diplomacy promotes "Japanese cultural traditions not as Japan's property but as the precious heritage of all humankind" and thus contributing to the preservation of world's cultural diversity (Ogoura, 2009, p. 52). Building peace is also one of its current directions. In addition, through a variety of public and private actors, Japan has been implementing public diplomacy initiatives to strengthen its positive image and cultural presence abroad as well as to nurture its international relations with various countries.

Specific features of Japan's public diplomacy

Various countries around the world have been conducting specific soft power or public diplomacy policies to enhance their presence abroad. China's "sharp power" is a case in point. The term "'sharp power' captures the malign and aggressive nature of the authoritarian projects, which bear little resemblance to the benign attraction of soft power" (Walker & Ludwig, 2017, p. 13). Through sharp power, "the generally unattractive values of authoritarian systems – which encourage a monopoly on power, top-down control, censorship, and coerced or purchased loyalty – are projected outward, and those affected are not so much audiences as victims" (Walker & Ludwig, 2017, p. 13).

In comparison with China or other countries worldwide, there are specific features that distinguish Japan's soft power and public diplomacy. There are two concepts that could be suggested to describe its uniqueness. First, from the viewpoint of its strategy, desired image, and cultural aspects communicated abroad, Japanese public diplomacy could be named "warm power" or "kind power". These terms illustrate Japan's policy since World War II, focused on the promotion of characteristic Japanese virtues, including the notions of *wa* (harmony), *omotenashi* (hospitality), and *omoiyari* (consideration) and cultural aspects like Japanese aesthetic sense, high mutual respect, philosophies, and traditions. Through these elements, Japan has been projecting an image of itself as a peace-loving, kind, and friendly country, which combines tradition with modernity. The new imperial era called Reiwa, where the character for *wa* is translated as "harmony" or "peace" in English, could also be considered another example of Japan's message to the world.

Second, from the perspective of its organization and structure emphasized in the prior sections, Japanese public diplomacy could also be named with the term "scattered power". This concept reflects the current state of Japan's public diplomacy, characterized by the lack of a common policy, as well as administratively by the absence of a central agency that would integrate the separate public and private actors and facilitate their projects.

Differently from China's sharp power, Japan's kind power is a clear example of soft power – "the use of positive attraction and persuasion to achieve foreign policy objectives", while "communicating compelling narratives" and "drawing on the resources that make a country naturally attractive to the world" (Portland, n.d.). In the Soft Power 30 index of 2019, the world's most comprehensive comparative assessment of global soft power, Japan stands in the eighth position and is Asia's highest-ranking country. This demonstrates the greater productivity of Japan's public diplomacy in comparison with other Asian countries like China and South Korea. However, to keep this tendency and achieve higher results in the future, it would be essential for Japan to work towards transforming its public diplomacy state of "scattered power" into a "unified power" policy. Applied in combination with its kind power, this unified power policy would further enhance the efficiency of Japan's public diplomacy and cultural presence abroad.

Main actors of Japan's public diplomacy: the Ministry of Foreign Affairs and the Japan Foundation

Currently there are two main actors in charge of Japanese public diplomacy – the Ministry of Foreign Affairs of Japan and the Japan Foundation.

MOFA's Public Diplomacy Department is engaged with external public relations, the promotion of Japanese language, studies, and culture abroad, and the conduct of people-to-people exchange as well as artistic and intellectual exchange. It also cooperates with the United Nations University and international organizations like UNESCO. At the same time, as Ogawa (2009, p. 271) points out, "there is no inter-ministerial coordination system within the Japanese government to discuss overall public diplomacy strategies or advise on resource allocation, performance, management, and evaluation".

MOFA conducts various public relations activities that introduce information on Japanese foreign policy through its own operations, embassies, and consular offices all over the world. Examples of such initiatives are the

> implementation of lectures, written contributions and appearance on local media by the staff of Japanese embassies and consulates including ambassadors and consuls-general, the issuance of newsletter and other information bulletin in local languages, the conduct of various Japanese cultural events, invitation programs for foreign opinion leaders, reporters and TV crews, the dispatch of Japanese experts/knowledgeable persons abroad to give lectures or contribute as panelists, and the production of publications and audiovisual materials in multiple languages.
>
> (MOFA, 2017)

It maintains various programs and projects on Japanese cultural promotion such as the *Web Japan* website for the comprehensive latest general information about Japan, the *Opinion Poll on Japan*, the *Japan Brand Program*, the *Japan House*, and the *Japan Creative Centre* for disseminating information on Japan's culture and technologies in Singapore.

Together with the public relations activities, MOFA carries out cultural exchange initiatives to "foster favorable and deep understanding of Japan's diplomatic policies and national circumstances" (MOFA, 2014). Such include the *Pop-Culture Diplomacy*, as well as the *Japanese Studies and*

Intellectual Exchange and the *Japanese Language Education* initiatives conducted through the Japan Foundation.

The second main actor for exercising Japanese public diplomacy is the Japan Foundation. It was established in October 1972 as a special legal entity supervised by the Ministry of Foreign Affairs and later, in October 2003, recognized as an independent administrative institution (The Japan Foundation, n.d.). It is considered Japan's "only institution dedicated to carrying out comprehensive international cultural exchange programs throughout the world" (The Japan Foundation, n.d.). The Japan Foundation functions with the aims to

> deepen understanding of Japan in foreign countries, promote mutual international understanding, contribute to the world in culture and other fields, create good international environment and contribute to the maintenance and development of harmonious foreign relations of Japan (Article 3, The Japan Foundation Independent Administrative Institution Law).
>
> (The Japan Foundation, 2003)

Through its close collaboration with MOFA, the Foundation acts as an intermediary between the government and the private and civil society sectors, while keeping a certain level of autonomy from the ministry (Ogawa, 2009, p. 272).

In addition to its headquarters located in Tokyo, the Japan Foundation has a Kyoto Office and two Japanese language institutes – the Japan Foundation Japanese-Language Institute, Urawa and the Japan Foundation Japanese-Language Institute Kansai. The Foundation has created a global network consisting of 25 overseas offices in 24 countries (including two Asia Center liaison offices) as well (The Japan Foundation, n.d.). It also cooperates with diverse Japanese language institutions and cultural exchange organizations all over the world. In addition, the Japan Foundation collaborates with Japanese embassies and consulates abroad for globally expanding its activities (The Japan Foundation, 2015).

The Japan Foundation carries out programs in three categories – art and cultural exchange, Japanese-language education overseas, and Japanese studies and intellectual exchange. The first category focuses on art and culture such as fine arts, performing arts, literature, films, food, and fashion. Through this program the Japan Foundation's objective is to create "opportunities for people all over the world to encounter Japanese art and culture by supporting artists, presenting works, and creating international networks" (The Japan Foundation, 2015, p. 2). In the second category, the Japan Foundation facilitates activities supporting Japanese language education abroad. Such programs include "organizing the Japanese-Language Proficiency Test, developing teaching materials, supporting Japanese courses, and providing training programs for Japanese-language teachers, as well as conducting worldwide surveys to meet the needs of all Japanese-language practitioners" (The Japan Foundation, 2015, p. 2). The third category centers on the provision of aid, which is granted through fellowships for research in Japan and through different grant programs. As part of this program, the Japan Foundation also carries out symposiums and collaborative projects to increase the interaction among experts in various countries (The Japan Foundation, n.d.).

In addition to the activities in the three main categories already introduced, the Japan Foundation also assists "individuals engaged in various cultural fields, and creates opportunities and supports programs end events, fostering sustained environments for cultural exchange" (The Japan Foundation, 2015, p. 5). For instance, it organizes international conferences focused on addressing global issues, international exhibitions and stage performances of Japanese and international artists, demonstrations of ikebana, tea ceremony, craft, cuisine, and other examples of Japanese culture, as well as invites researchers, teachers, and cultural figures from diverse countries (The Japan Foundation, 2015, p. 4). The Japan Foundation also provides funding to individuals involved in exhibitions and stage performances related to Japanese arts and culture and to people and non-profit organizations engaged in Japanese cultural exchange projects. Various universities and research institutes promoting Japanese studies, as well as programs assisting the professional skills of Japanese language teachers, also receive financial support from the Foundation (The Japan Foundation, 2015, p. 4). Some other activities of the Japan Foundation are to collect information and materials necessary for individuals in the field of cultural exchange and help them to develop their own networks. Such initiatives include "running online database of Japanese performing arts", "regularly issuing booklets in English highlighting Japanese books and films", "administering the Japanese-Language Proficiency Test (JLPT)", "developing online materials for teaching Japanese", "developing and deploying the JF Standard for Japanese-Language Education, a reference tool to help think about teaching, learning, and assessment in Japanese-language education", and "building international networks among scholars and intellectuals researching Japan" (The Japan Foundation, 2015, p. 5).

On the basis of a government endowment of 78 billion yen, the Japan Foundation's activities are financially supported by annual government subsidies, investment revenue, and donations from the private sector (The Japan Foundation, n.d.).

Other Japanese public diplomacy actors

Apart from the public diplomacy activities implemented by MOFA and the Japan Foundation, Japan exercises a rich palette of initiatives conducted by other public and private actors. One such example is the Cabinet Office and its Cool Japan Strategy, implemented in collaboration with various institutions.

Since the 1990s, a variety of patterns of "Japan-based entertainment as Japanimation, *manga* and electronic games have been enjoyed in many countries, and tasty, healthy Japanese food has attracted more and more people" (Minister in Charge of the "Cool Japan" Strategy, 2014). In the following years, the popularity of Japanese culture continued to grow in various countries all over the world. In 2002, Douglas McGray highlighted in his article the increasing global cultural influence of Japan, pointing out Japan's potential to become a cultural superpower in place of the economic preeminence that it had in the 1980s (McGray, 2002, p. 44). Coining the term "Gross National Cool", McGray stated that Japan "has become one of a handful of perfect globalization nations (along with the United States)" and its increasing cultural presence "has created a mighty engine of national cool" (McGray, 2002, p. 53).

Following the global interest in Japanese culture, around the notion of Japan as "cool", in 2002 the Japanese government started designing a new industrial policy that would become the "Cool Japan" strategy, an initiative launched in 2014 (Green, 2015, p. 59).

The Cool Japan Strategy is exercised by the Cabinet Office of the government in collaboration with various public and private actors. One such actor is the Ministry of Economy, Trade and Industry (METI), whose role is to "link the 'Cool Japan Initiative' to private business and spread them out to the world" (Ministry of Economy, Trade and Industry, 2014). The initiative covers the promotion of all aspects of Japanese culture "from subcultural products, such as *manga* and Japanimation, to traditional cultural heritage" (Cool Japan Movement Promotion Council, 2014, p. 2). For instance, the content could be "games, comics and cartons (*anime*), fashion, products, Japanese food, traditional culture, designs, and even such high-tech products as robots and environmental technologies" (Intellectual Property Strategy Headquarters, 2011, p. 33). The strategy's original purpose was to win "the sympathy of other countries toward Japan" (Cool Japan Movement Promotion Council, 2014, p. 2). However, despite the strong interest in Japanese culture around the world, it has been challenging for Japan to achieve the desired outcomes of the initiative. Some reasons have been the difficulties in understanding the concept of "Cool Japan" due to its broad meaning, causing certain criticism by the communities in each genre, and that the "system of attracting attention from outside Japan is also inadequate" (Cool Japan Movement Promotion Council, 2014, p. 2). Therefore, after some discussions, the Cool Japan Movement Promotion Council (hereinafter "the Council") transformed the original mission of the strategy to "Japan as a country that provides creative solutions to the world's challenges" (Cool Japan Movement Promotion Council, 2014, p. 5).

There are three main steps that Japan follows in order to achieve the Cool Japan Strategy's mission: "promoting domestic growth", "connecting Japan and other countries", and "becoming Japan that helps the world" (Cool Japan Movement Promotion Council, 2014, p. 6).

The first step – "promoting domestic growth" – consists of three missions: "acquiring skills for active communication with people overseas", "removing barriers to creativity and creating the trend of taking on challenges", and "supporting free attempts and cooperation without being restricted by a hierarchical structure or past examples" (Cool Japan Movement Promotion Council, 2014, p. 6). All these missions of the Cool Japan Strategy are achieved through particular actions proposed by the Council. For instance, in order to acquire skills for active communication with people over the world, there have been various activities to be implemented by Japan. Such include the holding of enjoyable Cool Japan classes for children, refining the Cool Japan study system abroad, promoting broadcasting with an English sub-audio channel, and establishing an English-speaking district where English is the official language (Cool Japan Movement Promotion Council, 2014, p. 7). To remove the barriers to creativity and create a trend of taking challenges, Japan should "promote the active recruitment of young people by Japanese companies and generational succession", "create a system of listeners to opinions on Cool Japan", "encourage creativity through deregulation", and "establish a Cool Japan intellectual property consultation center" (Cool Japan Movement Promotion Council, 2014, p. 7). To support free attempts and cooperation without being restricted by a hierarchical structure or past examples, Japan should "take on the challenge of new business based on creative cooperation among government offices", "promote a platform for government office cooperation", "support in-house entrepreneurs", and "support 100 new businesses that tackle issues facing Japan and the world" (Cool Japan Movement Promotion Council, 2014, p. 7).

The second step of the Cool Japan Strategy – "connecting Japan and other countries" – consists of three missions: "developing a better public image of Japan in the world", "increasing the mobility of information and cultural products of Japan in the international community", and "adopting overseas perspectives to discover the essential attractiveness of Japan" (Cool Japan Movement Promotion Council, 2014, p. 17). Following these missions, there are some particular actions proposed by the Council to be implemented by Japan. For example, in order to develop a better public image of Japan abroad, the country should "establish Japan's brand image and increase its overseas distribution", "create a new slogan that will replace Cool Japan", "disseminate the display of 'Designed in Japan'", and "review procurement to increase the government's creativity" (Cool Japan Movement Promotion Council, 2014, p. 17). To increase the mobility of information and cultural products of Japan in the international community, the country should "create Japan's inbound web portal", "translate signs at tourist sites into many languages with a pleasing appearance", and "support the translation of information given in Japanese" (Cool Japan Movement Promotion Council, 2014, p. 17). In order to adopt overseas perspectives to discover the essential attractiveness of Japan, the country should "appoint 100 partners who have an overseas perspective", "appoint Japanese persons working in the world as ambassadors", "understand and visualize the view of Japan from other countries, and expectations from Japan", and "analyze the demands of foreign tourists" (Cool Japan Movement Promotion Council, 2014, p. 17).

Similar to the former two steps outlined, the third step of the strategy's mission – "becoming Japan that helps the world" – consists of three missions: "personalizing the issues facing Japan and the world", "promoting industries through which Japan could contribute to the world in addressing such issues as environmental problems, a declining birthrate, and an aging population", and "delivering information on ancient Japanese philosophy that values sustainability and harmony" (Cool Japan Movement Promotion Council, 2014, p. 27). Again, certain activities are to be conducted by Japan to achieve the missions. For instance, to personalize the issues facing Japan and the world, the country should "visualize information on the issues" and "present the government's open data and incorporate design into government documents" (Cool Japan Movement Promotion Council, 2014, p. 27). To promote industries through which Japan could contribute to the world in tackling various global challenges, the country should "match problem-solving projects and creativity", "create an environment for the commercialization of ideas that will contribute to the world", and "promote the overseas expansion of problem-solving businesses" (Cool Japan Movement Promotion Council, 2014, p. 27). To present information on ancient Japanese philosophy that values sustainability and harmony, the country should "build JAPAN LABO across Japan", "hold international handicrafts festivals in Japan", "build a Japan design museum", and "expand Japan's cultivation of aesthetic sentiments enjoyed by children to the world" (Cool Japan Movement Promotion Council, 2014, p. 27).

In November 2013, the Japanese government demonstrated a significant financial investment through the establishments of a public-private fund named Cool Japan Fund, Inc., with the aim of "supporting and promoting the development of demand overseas for excellent Japanese products and services" (Cool Japan Fund Inc., 2018). The purpose of the fund is to "commercialize the 'Cool Japan' and increase overseas demand by providing risk capital for business across a variety of areas, including media & content, food & services, and fashion & lifestyle" (Cool Japan Fund Inc., 2018).

Apart from the Cabinet Office, another Japanese actor in charge of cultural promotion is the Agency for Cultural Affairs of the government. The Agency introduces Japanese culture abroad, participates in international cultural exchange, and "builds an international hub of creativity and information for culture and arts" (Agency for Cultural Affairs, n.d.). It also disseminates Japanese language, emphasizing the "importance of Japanese language education as the basis of Japanese culture" (Agency for Cultural Affairs, n.d.). In addition, by supporting Japanese language education programs, providing training for Japanese language teachers, and conducting certain surveys and studies, it assists foreigners living in Japan in their Japanese language studies. The Agency also encourages international cooperation in the protection of cultural properties by sending Japanese experts abroad as well as through the establishment of local human resources in countries around the world. It aims to "advance the arts and culture of Japan by encouraging mutual understanding with other countries, creating and reinforcing networks of cultural figures and artists, and prompting new artistic creation based on this exchange" (Agency for Cultural Affairs, n.d.). It conducts various programs and projects such as *Culture City of East Asia, Japan Cultural Envoy, Program to Create International Base for the Promotion of Arts and Culture (Support for Artists in Residence), International Exchange/Cooperation of Cultural Properties, The Year in International Exchange,* and *International Conferences on Culture.*

Another public diplomacy actor is the Japan National Tourism Organization (JNTO). Established in 1964, it carries out a variety of initiatives both domestically and overseas with the aim of attracting tourists from diverse countries to visit Japan. The JNTO's activities include "promotion of Japanese tourism", "operation of the Tourist Information Center in Japan for international visitors", "administration of Guide-interpreter examinations", "publication of tourism statistics and market reports", and "providing support for international conventions and incentive events" (JNTO, n.d.). JNTO also promotes tourism to Japan through its 20 offices, situated in cities around the world.

The Japan Tourism Agency of the Ministry of Land, Infrastructure, Transport and Tourism is another essential public diplomacy actor. Inaugurated in 2008, the Agency conducts various measures such as the *Visit Japan Campaign* to increase international tourism exchange. Its job is also to provide a "national environment friendly to tourist travel", which includes "creating appealing tourist destinations in Japan, upgrading tourism industries to fit traveler needs, promoting training and utilization of talent in the tourism field, encouraging the Japanese people to take vacations, and preparing safety measures for Japanese travelers abroad" (Japan Tourism Agency, n.d.).

Apart from the institutions already outlined, many other public and private organizations as well as NGOs are also exercising public diplomacy initiatives to strengthen Japanese soft power abroad. However, as Mori (2006, p. 48) highlights, "there is no expert who really understands and grasps the big picture of Japan's overall public diplomacy efforts". As was emphasized earlier, this is to a great extent due to the lack of coordination and integration among the variety of cultural promotion actors.

Notes

1 Japan also took part in expositions in Paris (1889), Melbourne (1875), Philadelphia (1876), Paris (1878), Sydney (1879), Berlin (1880), Atlanta (1881), Trieste (1882), Amsterdam (1883), St. Petersburg (1884), Nuremberg (1885), Barcelona (1888), Hamburg (1889), Chicago (1893), Paris (1900), Glasgow (1901), and Hanoi in French Indochina (1902).
2 The unequal treaties are described as "a series of treaties and agreements in which China was forced to concede many of its territorial and sovereignty rights" (The Editors of Encyclopaedia Britannica, n.d.). They were "negotiated during the 19th and early 20th centuries between China and foreign imperialist powers, especially Great Britain, France, Germany, the United States, Russia, and Japan" (The Editors of Encyclopaedia Britannica, n.d.).

References

Agency for Cultural Affairs. (n.d.). *Cultural exchange and international contributions*. Retrieved August 18, 2018, from www.bunka.go.jp/english/policy/international/

Cool Japan Fund Inc. (2018). *What is Cool Japan Fund?* Retrieved August 18, 2018, from www.cj-fund.co.jp/en/about/cjfund.html

Cool Japan Movement Promotion Council. (2014). Cool Japan proposal. *Cabinet Office*. Retrieved August 17, 2018, from www.cao.go.jp/cool_japan/english/pdf/published_document3.pdf

Green, H. (2015). The soft power of cool: Economy, culture and foreign policy in Japan. *Toyo University Repository for Academic Resources, 58*(2), 46–68.

Intellectual Property Strategy Headquarters. (2011, June 3). *Intellectual property strategic program 2011*. Retrieved August 18, 2018, from www.kantei.go.jp/jp/singi/titeki2/ipsp2011.pdf

Japan National Tourism Organization. (n.d.). *About JNTO*. Retrieved August 18, 2018, from www.japan.travel/en/about-jnto/

Japan Tourism Agency. (n.d.). *About the JTA*. Retrieved August 18, 2018, from www.mlit.go.jp/kankocho/en/about/index.html

Kaneko, M. (2007). Nihon no Paburikku Dipuromashi [Japanese public diplomacy]. In M. Kaneko & M. Kitano (Eds.), *Paburikku Dipuromashi* [Public diplomacy] (pp. 184–230). Tokyo, Japan: PHP Interface.

McGray, D. (2002, May/June). Japan's gross national cool. *Foreign Policy*, pp. 44–54. Retrieved from http://web.mit.edu/condry/Public/cooljapan/Feb23-2006/McGray-02-GNCool.pdf

Minister in Charge of the "Cool Japan" Strategy. (2014). *Declaration of Cool Japan's mission: Japan, a country providing creative solutions to the world's challenges.* Retrieved August 16, 2018, from www.cao.go.jp/cool_japan/english/pdf/published_document4.pdf

Ministry of Economy, Trade and Industry. (2014). *Cool Japan initiative.* Retrieved August 18, 2018, from www.meti.go.jp/policy/mono_info_service/mono/creative/file/1406CoolJapanInitiative.pdf

Ministry of Foreign Affairs of Japan. (2014, August 14). *Public diplomacy: Cultural exchange.* Retrieved August 2, 2018, from www.mofa.go.jp/policy/culture/exchange/index.html

Ministry of Foreign Affairs of Japan. (2017, July 11). *Public diplomacy: Public relations abroad.* Retrieved August 2, 2018, from www.mofa.go.jp/p_pd/pds/page24e_000149.html

Mori, S. (2006). *Japan's public diplomacy and regional integration in East Asia: Using Japan's soft power* (USJP Occasional Paper 06–10). Cambridge, MA: Program on US-Japan Relations, Harvard University.

Ogawa, T. (2009). Origin and Development of Japan's Public Diplomacy. In Snow, N. & Taylor, P. M. (Eds.), *Routledge Handbook of Public Diplomacy* (pp. 270–281). New York, NY and London: Routledge.

Ogoura, K. (2009). *Japan's Cultural Diplomacy, Past and Present.* Joint Research Institute for International Peace and Culture. Tokyo: Aoyama Gakuin University, 44–54.

Portland. (n.d.). What is soft power? *The Soft Power 30.* Retrieved November 25, 2020, from https://softpower30.com/what-is-soft-power/

The Editors of Encyclopaedia Britannica. (n.d.). Unequal treaty, Chinese history. *Encyclopaedia Britannica Online.* Retrieved August 21, 2021, from www.britannica.com/event/Unequal-Treaty

The Japan Foundation. (2003). *Organization.* Retrieved from www.jpf.go.jp/e/about/result/ar/2003/pdf/ar2003-03-01.pdf

The Japan Foundation. (2015). *Brochure "The Japan Foundation".* Retrieved from www.jpf.go.jp/e/about/outline/img/Pamphlet_e.pdf

The Japan Foundation. (n.d.). *About us.* Retrieved August 2, 2018, from www.jpf.go.jp/e/about/index.html

Walker, C., & Ludwig, J. (2017). *Sharp power, rising authoritarian influence: International forum for democratic studies.* Washington, DC: National Endowment for Democracy, pp. 8–25.

Watanabe, H. (2018). The new Japonisme: From international cultural exchange to cultural diplomacy – Evaluating the influence of cultural activities on diplomacy. Discuss Japan, Japan Foreign Policy Forum, Ministry of Foreign Affairs of Japan. *Diplomacy*, 50. https://www.japanpolicyforum.jp/diplomacy/pt201810301300038356.html

4   Japan's public diplomacy in Europe

The Japan Foundation in France and Bulgaria

To increase its relations with Europe and cultural presence on the continent, Japan has been exercising a variety of public diplomacy activities. The following section explores the Japanese cultural promotion initiatives in France and Bulgaria with an emphasis on the Japan Foundation. The section also observes other Japanese, Bulgarian, and French actors that have been acting autonomously or in collaboration with the Japan Foundation for introducing Japanese culture.

Promotion of Japanese culture in France: the Japan Foundation

Since the 1850s, there have been diverse Japanese cultural promotion activities in France, which even preceded Japan's first public diplomacy initiatives of the 1860s. Various cultural exchanges followed after the establishment of diplomatic relations between France and Japan in 1858, when the Treaty of Amity and Commerce was signed in Edo, the former Tokyo. This was during the Tokugawa period, the last era of traditional Japanese government before the Meiji Restoration of 1868.

The pioneer introducing Japanese culture and literature in France is the French ethnologist and linguist Leon de Rosny (Belouad, 2014, p. 215). Starting from the 1850s, he made a variety of contributions in the field.

In 1856, Rosny published his first work, called *Introduction à l'étude de la langue japonaise* (Introduction to the Study of Japanese Language). At the same time, he also took part in the activities of the Société asiatique[1] (Asian Society), particularly as a librarian. In addition, in 1859 Rosny participated in the foundation of the Revue orientale et américaine (American and Oriental Ethnographic Society), maintaining a career as both an orientalist and an ethnographer (Belouad, 2014, p. 218).

In the 1860s, Rosny contributed to the promotion of Japanese culture at another level – the institutionalization of Japanese studies in France.

DOI: 10.4324/9781003006251-4

In 1862, a delegation from the Japanese Embassy to Europe, also called Bunkyuu Embassy or Takenouchi Embassy, visited some European countries to negotiate the opening of certain Japanese ports, which were imposed by the so-called unequal treaties (Belouad, 2014, p. 220). The delegation went to France and spent about three weeks in Paris from April 7 to April 29, 1862. At the time, Rosny was appointed as an interpreter of the mission by the French government. During the visit of the mission, he established friendly relationships with some of the members, especially with Yukichi Fukuzawa, who in the following years was going to be an important intellectual and theoretician of the Japanese modernization, and with Munenori Terashima, who became the minister of foreign affairs of Japan in 1873. As a result, thanks to these two Japanese figures, France received the opportunity to obtain valuable knowledge on Japanese language, culture, and history (Belouad, 2014, pp. 220–221). Rosny's experience as an interpreter and the conversations with the mission also contributed much to the progress of his research on Japan.

From the perspective of the institutionalization of Japanese studies in France, the visit of the mission could be considered to have prompted the Ministry of Education to establish a Japanese language course in the country (Belouad, 2014, p. 221). In addition, highly contributory to the creation of the course was the development of the French-Japanese economic exchanges in the 1860s. The French government needed diplomats capable of speaking Japanese during the negotiations. Rosny was appointed as an interpreter and, following the request of the Ministry of Agriculture, he translated a Japanese treaty on the breeding of silkworms. In this political and economic context, in 1863 Rosny obtained authorization to open the first Japanese language course in France (Belouad, 2014, p. 221). In the beginning it was considered a free public course (*cours public et gratuit*), and five years later it received a more official status – a "chair of Japanese language" (*chaire de japonais*) at the Special School for Oriental Languages[2] (Belouad, 2014, p. 221).

In the 1860s, having never been to Japan, Rosny managed to build a reputable Japanese library in France. In the process of collecting materials, he was using European bookstores and auctions as well as relying on his personal network of Japanese people and foreigners living in Japan (Belouad, 2014, p. 226). In following years, Rosny made various other contributions as well. Such examples are the Japanese language textbooks, published in the course of his lectures at the Special School for Oriental Languages: *Exercices de lecture japonaise* (Japanese Reading Exercises) in 1863, *Recueil de textes japonais* (Collection of Japanese Texts) in 1863, *Grammaire japonaise* (Japanese Grammar) in 1865, and *Guide de la conversation japonaise* (Guide to Japanese Conversation) in 1865 (Belouad, 2014, p. 227). A few years later, two more textbooks were created by Rosny – *Thèmes faciles et gradués pour l'étude de la langue japonaise* (Easy and Advanced Themes for the Study of Japanese Language) in 1869, and *Manuel du style épistolaire et du style diplomatique* (Manual of the Epistolary and Diplomatic Style) in 1874. Among the aims of these textbooks was the provision of a Japanese language training for French diplomats, requested by the Ministry of Foreign Affairs (Belouad, 2014, p. 227).

Together with his teaching activities, Rosny published a large number of memoirs, articles, and books on Japan, mostly focused on its history. Such examples are the *Études asiatiques de géographie et d'histoire* (Asian Studies of Geography and History) in 1864, and the *Variétés orientales, historiques, géographiques, schientifiques, bibliographiques et littéraires* (Oriental, Historical, Geographical, Scientific, Bibliographic, and Literary Varieties) in 1868. In 1871, he also published a collection of Japanese poems translations entitled *Anthologie de poésie japonaise – Poésies ansiennes et modernes des insulaires du Nippon* (Anthology of Japanese Poetry – Ancient and Modern Poetry of the Nippon Islanders). In the same year, another contribution of Rosny was a script for a theatrical play called *Le Couvent du Dragon Vert* (The Green Dragon Convent).

In parallel with Rosny's activities introducing Japanese culture, in the 1860s Japan conducted its initial public diplomacy initiatives in France. The event, considered the first official presentation of Japan in France, is its participation in the World Exposition in Paris in 1867 (Lacambre, 1983, p. 298). Demonstrating diverse aspects of Japanese culture, the Japanese pavilion drew much interest from the French side. It consisted of a house with a straw roof and a couple of living rooms. In one of the rooms, a tea prepared in a Japanese manner was offered. There were also mannequins wearing Japanese costumes and a gallery with various shops.

In 1868, there was a big sale in Paris of 1308 Japanese objects, which were previously brought to France for the World Exposition in 1867. It consisted of precious works of art, collected from the "special museums" of Japanese princes (Lacambre, 1983, p. 298).

In the 1870s, Japan's participation in the Exposition in Paris highly contributed to French society's interest in Japanese art. Following the event was greater dissemination of knowledge and information on Japan (Belouad, 2014, p. 236). The gradual opening of Japan to the West also led to the appearance of various publications about the country. This growing interest in Japan is considered to have given birth to the Japonism in France. The term "Japonism" has been characterized with

> European craze for Japanese art – notably fans, screens, lacquers, bronzes, silks, porcelains and Ukiyo-e woodblock prints – which

arrived in huge quantities from Japan, following the decision taken in 1854 by the Tokugawa Shogunate to open up its seaports to international trade with the West.

(Encyclopedia of Art History, n.d.)

In France, the beginning of Japonism is associated with the deep appreciation of *ukiyo-e* woodblock prints in 1856, when the woodblock print artist Félix Henri Bracquemond was "astounded by the high artistic quality of Hokusai 'manga' prints stuffed as packaging into a box containing imported porcelain" (Watanabe, 2018).

Since the 1860s, the influence of Japanese arts could be noticed in various fields in France including decorative arts, fashion, theatre, literature, cinema, and arts. For instance, Claude Monet (1840–1926) applied elements of Japanese painting in both his portraiture and landscapes (Encyclopedia of Art History, n.d.). His work "Camille Monet in Japanese Costume" is a case in point. He designed a Japanese-style water garden at Giverny and painted numerous aquatic landscapes there as well. Japanese art was also a source of inspiration for Vincent Van Gogh (1853–1890) and various French poets and artists like Charles Baudelaire (1821–1867), Auguste Rodin (1840–1917), and Victor Hugo (1802–1885).

Between 1888 and 1891, a luxurious magazine in French, English, and German entitled *Le Japon Artistique* (Artistic Japan) was published by the critic and magazine writer Samuel Bing. It presented Japanese cultural elements such as *ukiyo-e*, ceramics, architecture, and *Kabuki* theater. The fact that the magazine was named "Artistic Japan" rather than "Japanese Art" demonstrates that "the life of the Japanese in its entirety was seen as artistic, and that admiration was directed towards Japan itself" (Watanabe, 2018).

In 1878, Japan participated in another exposition in Paris. Its presentation was abundant and neat and organized by Maeda Masana, a Japanese friend of France. The pavilion attracted the attention of the visitors with its interior characterized by simplicity and naturalness (Lacambre, 1983, p. 302). In 1889, Japan took part again in an exposition in France. This time at its pavilion there was a big gilded wood Buddha statue, brought from Nara. It was positioned at the entrance of an archaeology and anthropology sciences section, where various objects such as dolls, tea bowls, ceramics, combs, and masks were displayed.

The participation in expositions in France was part of Japan's general public diplomacy activities of "an 'undeveloped cultural nation' that were used to boost its profile as a new participant in an international society centered on the United States and Europe" (Watanabe, 2018). Japanese cultural initiatives were focused on presenting the nation both at home and overseas as a modernized country.

From the 1850s to the 1900s, Rosny's activities and Japanese public diplomacy initiatives provided French people with valuable knowledge regarding various aspects of Japanese culture such as its unique architecture, gardens, and works of art. France was enabled to know, perceive, and imagine Japan through these expositions as well as the available literature (Lacambre, 1983, p. 304). However, with the modernization of Japan and its transformation as a great Asian power during the Russo-Japanese War and World War I, the perceptions of Japan changed. Initially associated with "Japonisme's skill contained in simplicity, a gentle aesthetic couched in Asian exoticism", the impression of Japan turned into an image of an aggressive country (Watanabe, 2018). These negative perceptions continued during World War II, leading to the decrease of Japanese cultural popularity in France. As Watanabe (2018) highlights, "the Oriental fashion that was called 'Japonisme' lost its freshness and passed its best before date".

In the 1950s and the early 1960s, Japanese cultural initiatives in France developed in new dimensions with the purpose of transforming the prewar image of Japan into one of a peace-loving country. In the following years, Japanese public diplomacy focused on the reestablishment of the positive perceptions and high cultural presence in France. Japan's goal was to project itself as a harmonious and economically advanced nation.

In 1953, the governments of Japan and France signed a bilateral cultural agreement providing many opportunities for cultural exchanges between the two countries. The agreement also created a favorable atmosphere for Japanese cultural promotion in France. Following this, in the 20th and 21st centuries, there has been a rich palette of public diplomacy initiatives, introducing Japanese traditional and contemporary culture, as well as Japan's technologies and innovations. The purpose of these activities is to present Japan in a new light as a technologically advanced and peaceful country that combines tradition with modern culture. These initiatives have been highly contributory to the restoration of interest in Japanese culture and Japan's presence in France.

Since 1973, crucial public diplomacy actor introducing Japanese culture in France has been the Japan Foundation. It has been implementing a variety of programs in the following three categories – art and cultural exchange, Japanese-language education, and Japanese studies and intellectual exchange. The projects have been exercised autonomously by the Japan Foundation, in cooperation with various public and private actors, as well as through the provision of financial support to individuals and organizations participating in the Foundation's programs.

Art and cultural exchange

In the art and cultural exchange field, the Japan Foundation has been carrying out a rich palette of public diplomacy activities in France both autonomously and in collaboration with Japanese and French public and private actors. Such an example is the program initiated in 1974 for introducing Japanese culture abroad (*Nipponbunka Shōkai Haken*), characterized by the provision of financial assistance for dispatching Japanese artists and cultural figures to conduct activities aimed at presenting aspects of Japanese traditional and contemporary culture in France. In the 1970s, such activities included lectures on *gagaku* classical music, Japanese contemporary music, and contemporary Japanese houses, performances of music and the *koto* musical instrument, and lectures and demonstrations of the *shamisen* musical instrument and the *go* game. The Foundation also conducted surveys at French organizations on the cultural exchange and the current state of the Japanese and Southeast Asian studies in Europe. A survey on the Japanese language education at national language educational institutions in France was carried out as well. In addition, the Foundation held discussions with French organizations on the promotion of cultural exchange between the two countries. In the following years, many activities have been implemented as part of the program. For instance, in the 1980s there were demonstrations of tea ceremony and *origami* paper folding, a presentation of research on Taoist and Buddhist studies in Japan, lectures on Japanese theater like *Kabuki* theater, *go* game guidance, and screenings of animation films. The Foundation also conducted lectures on Japanese culture in France in collaboration with French educational institutions. The "Formation and Development of the Modern Japanese Civilization" lecture, hosted by the College de France, is a case in point. The Foundation organized the "Regional Development in Japan" lecture in cooperation with the Lille 2 University of Health and Law as well. Apart from these lectures, in the 1980s, it dispatched professional staff to France to assist with the restoration of the Japanese garden at the UNESCO headquarters in Paris. In addition, in 1985, a Japanese Culture and Information Center was established at the Japanese Embassy in France. To celebrate the event, with the assistance of the Japan Foundation, a tearoom, donated by Urasenke, was assembled in France. In the 1990s, 2000s, and 2010s, the program's initiatives were enriched with symposiums on Japanese ceramics, lectures on *ikebana* flower arrangement, Japanese cuisine, animation, the Japanese silk industry and technology, a lecture and a workshop on *manga* comic books, demonstration of *sencha* tea, co-productions and exhibitions of artworks, and performances of *wadaiko* drums and Japanese dance and music, providing the French public with opportunities to experience Japan from diverse perspectives.

Since 1982, as part of another program entitled "Overseas Japanese Film Festival", the Japan Foundation has been holding annual film festivals in France. In the organization of the events, it has been collaborating with Japanese and French institutions such as the Japanese Embassy and the French film organization Cinematheque Francaise. The Foundation has been providing Japanese feature films and animations to the Japanese Embassy and the Japan Cultural Institute in Paris, aimed at presenting both traditional and contemporary Japanese culture. At the same time, to contribute further to the strengthening of the Japanese cultural presence in France, since the 1980s, the Foundation has been taking part in international film festivals in France, such as the Rennes Film Festival.

In the field of Japanese literature promotion in France, the Japan Foundation has been playing a highly essential role. Since the 1980s, it began providing financial assistance for the translation and publication of Japanese language textbooks and books introducing Japanese culture in France. The initiative continues at present, enabling the French public to further develop their image and knowledge on Japanese culture.

In addition to the *Nipponbunka Shōkai Haken* program, the Japan Foundation has been implementing various other programs and initiatives for cultural promotion in France through providing grants for dispatching performance groups, artists, and works of art, as well as through supporting Japan's participation in international exhibitions and festivals in France. For instance, in the 1970s, performances of *Bunraku* puppet theater, traditional Japanese dances, and *gagaku* classical music, as well as exhibitions of modern Japanese dyeing, children's books, and the "Toshodaiji Temple Exhibition", were organized with the Foundation's assistance in France. At the same time, Japan took part in the Biennale de Paris international art festival. In the 1980s, performances of *Noh* theater, *kyogen* traditional comic theater, the Tokyo Philharmonic Orchestra, and Japanese contemporary music, and a variety of sculpture and art exhibitions, were also held. In the 1990s, the Japan Foundation supported the organization of exhibitions in France dedicated to Japonism as well as a large exhibition on the topic "Treasures of Japanese Buddhism" (*Nihon bukkyō no hōko*). Thanks to its support, Japan also participated in the Avignon Festival, a widely popular arts festival held in the French city of Avignon every summer.

In May 1997, the Japan Foundation's Japan Cultural Institute in Paris (*Maison de la culture du Japon à Paris*) (MCJP) opened in France. It has been considered a highly essential Japanese cultural promotion institution in France, utilized as a "place to introduce Japanese culture, promote Japanese language and implement dialogue between Japan and France or Europe" (Ministry of Foreign Affairs of Japan, 2020). The Institute represents the Japan Foundation and its activities, which are organized in cooperation with the Association for the Japan Cultural Institute in Paris. It is focused on presenting both Japanese traditional and contemporary culture in France. The Institute's activities include exhibitions, live shows, cinema, conferences, and more recently promotion of Japanese language and culinary culture (Maison de la culture du Japon à Paris, 2019). Various courses on tea ceremony, calligraphy, *ikebana* flower arrangement, *origami* paper folding, and *manga* comic books have been hosted as well. In addition, the Institute offers a library with a variety of literature on Japan.

Since the establishment of the Institute, the Japan Foundation has been providing grants for dispatching Japanese intellectuals to France to conduct lectures on Japanese culture both at the Institute and at French institutions. For instance, in the 1990s there were lectures on the culture of Okinawa, *kyogen* traditional comic theater, Japanese traditional music, dance, and musical instruments, Japanese gardens and contemporary art, science, and technology, and the "Contemporary Japanese Manga" lecture.

In the 2000s and the 2010s, the number of the Japanese cultural promotion activities implemented by the Japan Foundation both autonomously and in collaboration with Japanese and French public diplomacy actors increased in France. For instance, there were Japanese musical concerts, sponsored by the Waseda University's Tsubouchi Memorial Theatre Museum, a college exchange project, organized together with the French agency Campus France, and an *ukiyo-e* prints exhibition, held in cooperation with UNESCO. The Japan Foundation has also been supporting and participating in the Japan Expo event in France through various initiatives including stage performances, presentations, and film screenings. At the same time, in the 2000s and the 2010s, it continued to dispatch specialists in the fields of visual and performing arts and to take part in international exhibitions and festivals with the aim of introducing both traditional and contemporary Japanese culture in France. For instance, there were demonstrations of martial arts, performances of contemporary dances, exhibitions of *manga* comic books, fashion, and Japanese contemporary architecture, as well as photo exhibitions of Japanese landscapes, a symposium on the Japanese postwar society, *origami* paper folding atelier, and fairs on study abroad programs in Japan. The Foundation also assisted Japan's participation in the Lyon Dance Biennale and the Lyon Biennale of Contemporary Art. In addition, it invited French representatives to participate in cultural events held in Japan such as contemporary dance festivals, a large-scale *ukiyo-e* prints exhibition in 2004, the "Art and Technology Exhibition" in 2003, and other exhibitions on Japanese arts.

Since the 2000s, together with the Foundation's activities emphasized previously, the Japan Cultural Institute in Paris has been implementing and co-sponsoring a variety of Japanese cultural initiatives in France both autonomously and in collaboration with Japanese and French public diplomacy actors like the Japanese Embassy, the Tokyo National Museum, the JNTO, the National Institute of Oriental Languages and Civilizations (INALCO), French and Japanese museums, and others. For example, in the 2000s and the 2010s such activities included tea ceremony and calligraphy courses, performances of Japanese theater and traditional and contemporary music, lectures on Japanese cuisine, demonstrations of *ikebana* flower arrangement and martial arts, a demonstration and a symposium on robots and a robot contest as part of the "People and Robots" exhibition in 2003, screenings of Japanese documentary and animation films, an exhibition of ceramics and the "Paper and Japonism" exhibition in 2006. In 2009, the Institute also held the "Japan Pop Culture Festival" in France, offered a venue for the conduct of an event introducing Japanese food ingredients, sponsored by the JETRO France, and hosted a meeting of the French-Japanese friendship associations throughout France. As part of its grant projects, it provided assistance for the organization of the Japan Cultural Festival (*Nihon Bunka Matsuri*) in 2009 in Avignon city as well. In addition, it has been supporting the implementation of various Japanese language speech contests for French high school, college, and university students in the country.

Since the 2010s, the Japan Foundation has been conducting a special program for promoting the understanding of Japanese contemporary culture in France (*Gendainihon Rikai Tokubetsu Puroguramu*) in collaboration with various French institutions. For instance, together with INALCO and the Paris Diderot University it has been establishing new courses, conducting lectures on Japan, and hiring young researchers.

In 2018, in cooperation with Japanese and French public diplomacy actors, the Japan Foundation played a great role in the implementation of the large-scale project "Japonismes 2018: *les âmes en resonance*" (Japonismes 2018: souls in resonance) in France. The project was held jointly by Japan and France to commemorate the 160th Anniversary of the establishment of the diplomatic relations between the two countries. As was highlighted previously, in the 19th century, Japonism "spread rapidly after *ukiyo-e* and other aspects of Japanese culture were introduced to France, having great influence on artists such as van Gogh and Claude Monet" (Japonismes 2018, 2018). Since then, various Japanese cultural elements have been presented in France, achieving much appreciation among the French society. In 2018, Japonism was characterized to be "gaining popularity once again, inspired by the creativity of modern day Japan, which still has the power to surprise and attract" (Japonismes 2018, 2018).

The Japonismes 2018 was an eight-month large-scale project, consisting of an official program of events like exhibitions and stage performances at nearly 100 venues in Paris, aimed at demonstrating various forms of

Japanese culture. The diversity of Japan's culture was introduced through "presentations ranging from works of the ancient Jomon period that is the origin of Japanese culture, Ito Jakuchu, and Rinpa School painting; to the latest media arts, animation, and comics; as well as *Kabuki*, contemporary drama, and Hatsune Miku performances" (Japonismes 2018, 2018). The project also provided opportunities for participation in cultural exchange programs with themes derived from the Japanese daily life, including Japanese cuisine and traditional regional festivals. In addition, the Japonismes 2018 Official Program was accompanied by Japonismes 2018 Associate Program, consisting of other Japan-related activities and events conducted in France in line with Japonismes 2018.

In charge of the general management of the project was the Ministry of Foreign Affairs of Japan, while the planning and implementation was exercised by the Japan Foundation, which acted as a secretariat for Japonismes 2018. The Foundation coordinated the project's initiatives in cooperation with various public and private institutions, including Japanese and French ministries and agencies. In Japan, such institutions were the Ministry of Foreign Affairs, the Japan Tourism Agency, the Ministry of Economy, Trade and Industry, the Ministry of Agriculture, Forestry and Fisheries (MAFF), the Agency for Cultural Affairs, the National Tax Agency, the Ministry of Internal Affairs and Communications (MIC), the Intellectual Property Strategy Promotion Bureau, and the secretariat of the HQ for the Tokyo Olympic and Paralympic Games. In France, the project was coordinated by the Japan Foundation and its Japan Cultural Institute in Paris together with the Japanese Embassy and the Ministry of Foreign Affairs from the Japanese side, and the Ministry of Foreign Affairs and International Development (MFAID) of France, *Élysée Palace* (Elysium Boutique Hotel), MCC, and City of Paris from the French side (Japonismes 2018, 2018).

During the Japonismes 2018 event, together with its function as a secretariat, the Japan Foundation also supported the organization of stage performances, exhibitions of Japanese arts, crafts, *manga* comic books, animation and games, and other activities in France. In addition, the Japan Cultural Institute in Paris hosted some official programs and offered the Japonismes 2018 Information Centre, which was set up on its ground floor during the event. The Center provided information regarding the schedule and the venue of the official programs as well as incorporated a "space for events and exhibitions related to the official program for visitors to gain a deeper understanding of the program" (Japonismes 2018, 2018).

Thanks to the integrated efforts of the Japan Foundation and the other actors involved, the Japonismes 2018 initiative presented a rich variety of aspects introducing Japanese traditional and contemporary culture. According to the Ministry of Foreign Affairs of Japan (2019), the event was characterized as "an all-Japan project implemented through public-private cooperation with the aim of contributing to spreading the attractiveness of Japan's regions, promoting inbound tourism, and expanding the export of Japanese products overseas, while looking ahead to the Olympic and Paralympic Games Tokyo 2020".

Japanese-language education

The Japan Foundation has been exercising various public diplomacy initiatives for Japanese language promotion in France. For instance, since 1974, it has been implementing a program for dispatching short-term and long-term Japanese language and culture specialists as well as visiting Japanese professors to educational institutions in France. From the 1980s, the Foundation has also been conducting training programs for non-native Japanese language teachers in France, enabling them to improve both their Japanese language skills and teaching methodology.

Since the 1970s, the Japan Foundation has been organizing a Japanese language training in Japan for French students with excellent performance in their Japanese language studies. The training aims to encourage Japanese language learning in France and contributes to the deepening of the French students' knowledge on Japanese language and culture. In addition, from the 1980s, the Foundation has been conducting various other grant projects offering Japanese language trainings in Japan. One such example is the initiated in 2000 Japanese language training for French university graduate students and researchers (*Daigakuinsei Nihongo Kenshū*). Since 2005, a training for French experts who need to acquire Japanese language skills for their research activities or professional career (*Senmon Nihongo Kenshū*) has been held as well.

Together with the initiatives above, since the 1990s, the Japan Foundation has been conducting a grant program for supporting Japanese language and culture education activities at French institutions and organizations. Such institutions include the Fondation France Libertés – Danielle Mitterrand, the French National Center for Scientific Research, the Paris Nanterre University, the University of Toulouse-Jean Jaurès, and others. Since 1992, the Foundation has also been subsidizing the implementation of the Japanese-Language Proficiency Test in the country. In addition, it has been administering a grant program for funding the organization of Japanese language speech contests (*Kaigai Nihongo Benrontaikai Josei)*.

To promote Japanese language in France, the Japan Foundation has been donating Japanese language teaching materials to various institutions in the country. In the 1970s, such institutions included the University of Lyon and the Jean Moulin University Lyon 3. In the 1980s, teaching materials were also provided to INALCO, the Paris Diderot University, and the Lille 1 University of Science and Technology. In the following years, the number of institutions expanded to include the University of Strasbourg, the Bordeaux Montaigne University, the University of Rennes 2, the University of Paris VIII, and others.

The Japan Foundation's Japan Cultural Institute in Paris has also been implementing various activities in the field of Japanese language promotion in France. It has been offering Japanese language courses at diverse levels, as well as hosting Japanese language education guidance and workshops both autonomously and in cooperation with other public diplomacy actors like the European Association for Japanese Studies (EAJS).

Japanese studies and intellectual exchange

The Japan Foundation has been carrying out a variety of public diplomacy initiatives to promote Japanese studies and intellectual exchange in France. The grant program for supporting international collaborative research projects is a case in point. Since the 1970s, the Foundation has been providing subsidies to conduct seminars and symposiums on various topics in collaboration with Japanese and French educational institutions. For instance, in the 1990s such topics were the cultural exchange promotion between Japan and Europe, the economic relations between Europe and East Asia, and the unresolved regional conflicts and nuclear issues after the Cold War. In the 2000s, issues like the EU-Japan cooperation in economics, politics and security, culture and globalization, and the business ethics and corporation governance were also discussed. In 2012, an international conference on *manga* comic books and animation was held in France as well. Many of these symposiums have been hosted by the Japan Cultural Institute in Paris. Such examples are the symposium on Japanese politics in 2009 and the symposiums on the topic "Japan · Cool", organized in collaboration with the Paris Institute of Political Studies' Center for International Studies (CERI) in 2006 and 2007. The Institute has been conducting symposiums on Japanese studies as well.

As part of its public diplomacy initiatives, the Japan Foundation has been administering programs for supporting Japanese studies organizations in France. Since the 1970s, it has been subsidizing French institutions offering Japanese studies and conducting research activities on Japan. Such institutions are the Paris Diderot University, the Paris Institute of Political Studies, the University of Rennes 1's Graduate School of Management, the Lyon 2 University's Institute of East Asian Studies, the French Society of Japanese Studies (*Société française des études japonaises*), and others. In addition, to promote Japanese studies and culture in France, from the 1980s the

Foundation has been donating books on Japan to the Japanese Culture and Information Center at the Japanese Embassy as well as to French institutions including the College de France, the Paris Diderot University, the New Sorbonne University Paris 3, the University of Rennes 1's Graduate School of Management, the Aix-Marseille University, the University of Lyon, the Jean Moulin University Lyon 3, the Bordeaux Montaigne University, the University of Toulouse-Jean Jaurès, the Lille 1 University of Science and Technology, the Lille 3 Charles de Gaulle University, the Ecole Polytechnique, INALCO, the National Library of France, the Guimet Museum of Asian Art, and others.

To develop specialists on Japan in France and to strengthen the Japanese research network, since 1974 the Japan Foundation has been carrying out the Japanese Studies Fellowship Program, offering research fellowships to Japanese studies scholars in diverse fields like Japanese politics, culture, economics, and others. Thanks to this program, French researchers have been receiving the opportunity not only to conduct research at Japanese universities, but also to enhance their understanding of Japanese culture and establish various relationships. In addition, the Japan Foundation has been administering invitation programs for French scholars, experts, and special guests. For instance, in 2016 it invited French art journalists to Japan to encourage interest in Japanese art and to contribute to the dissemination of information on Japanese art in France.

Since 2016, to promote Japanese contemporary culture, the Japan Foundation has been cooperating with the Ministry of Foreign Affairs on the implementation of the "International MANGA Award" initiative in France through inviting the awardees to Japan. From 1988, it has also been offering an "International Exchange Encouragement Prize" to French people who have demonstrated outstanding achievements in the field of international cultural exchange and Japanese cultural promotion.

Promotion of Japanese culture in Bulgaria: the Japan Foundation

It is believed that Japanese cultural promotion in Bulgaria was initiated with the first book on Japan by Anton Bozukov in 1906, a travel diary in which he outlines his experience in Japan and impressions about Japanese culture and people. With this work, Bozukov also started the tendency of Bulgarians writing travel diaries after visiting Japan (Petkova, 2012, p. 2).

The first official partnership between Bulgaria and Japan was created in 1939 when both countries established their diplomatic missions on each other's territories (Embassy of Japan in Bulgaria, n.d.). In addition, in 1930 the first literary translations were also created, and thus "political and cultural interaction went hand in hand" (Petkova, 2012, p. 2). Such translations included Japanese poetry like *Yamato-no Uta* (Pesni ot Yamato) and *Hana-no Eda* (Tsufnala veika) by Nikola Jerov. The first book on Japanese literature named *Japanese Literature: Beginnings, Development, Authors* (Yaponska literatura: nachalo-razvitie-predstaviteli) was also published in 1941 by Svetoslav Minkov (Petkova, 2012, p. 2). Later, in the 1950s and the 1960s, works of Tokunaga Sunao, Abe Kōbō, and Kawabata Yasunari that were translated from other European languages became widely admired in Bulgaria as well.

On February 11, 1943, the first official document regarding bilateral cultural relations – Agreement on Friendship and Cultural Cooperation – was signed in Tokyo by the Bulgarian Plenipotentiary Minister Yanko Peev and the Japanese Foreign Minister Masayuki Tani (Vutova-Stefanova, 2016, p. 139). Although this agreement became invalid when diplomatic relations were interrupted from 1944 to 1959 as a result of the impact of the World War II, the countries continued their intercultural interactions. In 1975, a new agreement on cooperation in science, art, and culture between the governments of Bulgaria and Japan was signed, providing a variety of opportunities for cultural exchange initiatives, which continue at present. Under the contract, both governments agreed to collaborate on the exchange of experts, scientists, students, athletes, and others engaged in cultural activities, on the provision of scholarship for education and research at the respective universities and educational institutions, as well as on the sharing of informational materials, books, magazines, and others (Kandilarov, 2012, p. 2).

In the following years, Japanese cultural promotion activities increased in Bulgaria. For instance, between 1972 and 1994, seven books on Japan were published by Bulgarian writers, journalists, diplomats, and Japanese studies specialists[3] (Petkova, 2012, p. 3). In their works, the authors shared their experiences and impressions after visiting Japan. As Petkova (2012, p. 3) points out, "because of their power to raise public awareness of Japan's culture and achievements, these books collectively functioned to increase reception of Japanese culture during this period". In addition, in 1977 the first two literary masterpieces translated directly from Japanese – *Yuki Guni* and *Senba-Zuru* by Kawabata Yasunari – also became available for Bulgarian readers. In the following 25 years, Japanese literature continued to serve as an essential instrument for introducing Japanese culture in Bulgaria. Various works of Akutagawa Ryūnosuke, Ōe Kenzaburō, Tanizaki Junichirō, Tsuboi Sakae, Ibuse Masuji, Mishima Yukio, Shiga Naoya, Arishima Takeo, Sei Shōnagon, and others were translated by Japanese studies specialists, providing the Bulgarian public with deeper insight into Japanese culture, philosophy, aesthetics, and social issues (Petkova, 2012, p. 3).

At the time, the intercultural cooperation between Bulgaria and Japan continued to increase, providing a favorable atmosphere for Japan's cultural promotion initiatives in the country. One such example is the "Japanese Calligraphy and Ink Painting" exhibition held in 1981 at the National Library "St. Cyril and Methodius" in Sofia, Bulgaria. To take part in the event, a delegation from the Japan Calligraphy Museum led by the president of the Japan Art Academy, Professor Jirō Arimitsu, and the director of the museum, Koyama Tenshū, arrived in Bulgaria. A movie about the history of calligraphy, lectures on Japanese literature and writing, and demonstrations of calligraphy by Japanese calligraphers were also presented during the exhibition (Kandilarov, 2012, pp. 11–12). The event is considered highly contributory to the deepening of the Bulgarian people's interest in Japanese culture.

In the following years, Japanese public diplomacy activities continued to increase in the country. A crucial contributor has been the Japan Foundation, working both autonomously and together with essential public and private actors in the field of Japanese cultural promotion. Since an office of the Japan Foundation has not been established in the country yet, the Japanese Embassy has been facilitating its programs and activities.

The Japan Foundation's first initiatives in the country began in the 1970s. It was a period characterized by rich cultural exchange between the two countries. In addition, the agreement on cooperation in science, art, and culture between the governments of Bulgaria and Japan of 1975 played a vital role in the creation of a favorable atmosphere for the Japan Foundation's public diplomacy activity in Bulgaria. It provided a variety of opportunities for Japanese cultural promotion initiatives. At the time, the president of the Foundation, Kon Hidemi, actively participated during the debates for the agreement (Kandilarov, 2016, p. 115). One month after finalizing the agreement, a Bulgarian delegation, led by Lyudmila Zhivkova, the chair of the Committee for Art and Culture, visited Japan. The delegation negotiated with the Japan Foundation the organization of a variety of activities on the two countries' territories, such as exhibitions in the field of painting, folklore and applied arts, musical exchange, as well as a reception of Bulgarian specialists in Japan through the assistance of the Foundation (Kandilarov, 2016, p. 115). In 1976, following an invitation by the Committee for Art and Culture, two cultural delegations led by Kon Hidemi and Professor Egami Namio also arrived in Bulgaria to discuss various initiatives and mechanisms for further cooperation on cultural exchange between the two countries (Kandilarov, 2016, pp. 115–116). As a result, Bulgarian-Japanese cultural interactions increased and a broad range of projects of the Japan Foundation has been conducted in Bulgaria.

The Japan Foundation's initiatives in Bulgaria could be classified in three categories – art and cultural exchange, Japanese-language education, and

Japanese studies and intellectual exchange. The projects have been carried out autonomously by the Japan Foundation, in cooperation with various public and private actors, as well as through the provision of financial support to individuals and organizations participating in the Foundation's programs.

Art and cultural exchange

The Japan Foundation's first public diplomacy projects in Bulgaria in the field of art and cultural exchange began with an *ikebana* flower arrangement demonstration in 1974, as part of its program for introducing Japanese culture abroad (*Nipponbunka Shōkai Haken*). The program has been characterized by the provision of financial assistance for dispatching Japanese artists and cultural figures to conduct activities aimed at presenting aspects of Japanese traditional and contemporary culture. For instance, in the 1990s such initiatives included performances of *kyogen* traditional comic theater, a concert of *shamisen*, *shakuhachi*, and *kotsudzumi* musical instruments, and a lecture entitled "Postwar Japanese Economy and Economic Policy" given by a Japanese specialist at the University of National and World Economy in Sofia. In the 2000s, a *Butoh* dance theater workshop was also held. In the 2010s, there was an *ukiyo-e* prints demonstration and a lecture and demonstration of the Niigata's cuisine, presenting the history of rice making in Niigata prefecture.

Apart from the *Nipponbunka Shōkai Haken* program, both autonomously and in collaboration with Japanese and Bulgarian public diplomacy actors, the Japan Foundation has been implementing various other programs and initiatives for cultural promotion in Bulgaria through providing grants for dispatching performance groups, artists, and works of art, as well as through supporting Japan's participation in international exhibitions and festivals in Bulgaria. For example, in the 1970s, demonstrations of *judo* and *ikebana*, performances of Japanese songs, traditional dances, and the *koto* musical instrument, and exhibitions of contemporary Japanese color photography and *ukiyo-e* prints were arranged with the Foundation's assistance. In the 1980s, the "Contemporary Japanese Ceramics Exhibition", the "Japanese Contemporary Architecture" photo exhibition, and demonstrations of *judo* and *origami* paper folding were also held in Bulgaria. In addition, the Foundation supported Japan's participation in the "Sofia International Book Exhibition". In the 1990s, there were lectures on calligraphy, *kirie* Japanese paper cutting, demonstrations of martial arts and *sado* tea ceremony, a *shakuhachi* musical instrument concert, performances of *wadaiko* drums, Japanese traditional music, and *Noh* theater, the "Traditional Ceramics Exhibition", and others. In the 2000s and the 2010s, the Foundation supported the organization of the "Contemporary Japanese Crafts Exhibition" as well as lectures and demonstrations of *Kabuki* theater and *sumo*, a lecture and a workshop on the Japanese traditional sweets *wagashi*, and performances of *Rakugo* storytelling, classical music, Japanese contemporary dance, and others. At the same time, in 2006, in collaboration with the Fukuyama Bulgaria Association and the Global Cultural Center, the Japan Foundation held an international exhibition on contemporary art in the city of Kazanluk in Bulgaria. In 2011, together with the Fukuyama Bulgaria Association, the Foundation also arranged Japanese music concerts of *koto*, *shakuhachi*, and *shamisen* musical instruments. In 2012, in cooperation with the Japanese Embassy, it organized a workshop and performance of *Noh* theater as well.

In addition to the activities emphasized previously, the Japan Foundation has been implementing and co-sponsoring a variety of other Japanese cultural initiatives in Bulgaria both autonomously and in collaboration with Japanese and Bulgarian public diplomacy actors. One such example is the large-scale annual event called "Days of Japanese Culture" (*Nihon Bunka Gekkan*). The event has been conducted in Bulgaria since 1991 by the Japanese Embassy with the support of the Japan Foundation and other public and private actors, including Nihon-tomono-kai, the Club of the Friends of Japan in Bulgaria, museums, galleries, and academic institutions, business enterprises, clubs, associations and foundations related to Japanese cultural promotion, and others. The Foundation has been providing Japanese feature films for "Japan Film Week", held every year at the "Days of Japanese Culture" with the aim of increasing Bulgarian people's understanding of Japan. Since the 1990s, the Japan Foundation has been assisting in the organization of various other initiatives, introducing Japanese culture in Bulgaria such as concerts of *koto* and *shakuhachi* musical instruments, Japanese music, performances of *wadaiko* drums and the *tsugaru shamisen* musical instrument by the group "Bu-Shi-Do", *Noh* theater, exhibitions of calligraphy, demonstrations of *ikebana*, and lectures on Japanese ceramics. In 2015, the two-day annual festival "Aniventure", presenting elements of Japanese traditional and contemporary culture, was arranged with the support of the Foundation as well.

In the field of Japanese literature promotion in Bulgaria, the Japan Foundation has been playing a highly essential role. Since the 1980s, it has been providing financial assistance for the translation and publication of a rich variety of works by classic and contemporary authors introducing Japanese culture in the country. In the 1980s, such examples are *Makura no Soushi* (Zapiski pod Vuzglavkata) by Sei Shōnagon and *Aruonna* (Jena) by Arishima Takeo. In the 1990s, published with the Foundation's support were also the books *Suna no Onna* (Jenata ot Pyasucite) by Abe Kōbō, *Kagi* (Klyuchut) by Tanizaki Junichirō, *Watashino Anne Furanku* (Moyata Ane Frank) by Matsutani Miyoko, *Haiku* (Haiku) by Galina Tomova-Stankeva, and *Kicchin* (Kuhnyata) by Yoshimoto Banana. In addition, between 2000 and 2009, the Foundation provided financial aid for publishing the books *Zaetostta v Yaponiya* (Nihon no Koyou) by Pobeda Vasileva Loukanova, *Nihon no Gendai Kenchiku wo Ōku no Shashin to Tomoni Shoukai Shita Hon* (Architectural Spies: Japan) in English, Bulgarian, and Japanese by Nadya Stamatova and Scott Pierson Skipworth, as well as the Bulgarian translation of the book *Matsu no Kaze: Hotoke kyou Bunka to shite no Sadou Koten yori no Kaisetsu Yakuchū* (Vyatur v Klonite na Bora) by Hirota Dennis. In the 2010s, there was also translation assistance for the Bulgarian versions of the books *Kazoku Hakkei* (Semeini Sceni) by Tsutsui Yasutaka, *Shikisai wo Motanai Tazaki Tsukuruto, Kare no Junrei no Toshi* (Bezcvetniyat Tsukuru Tadzaki i Negovite Godini na Stranstvane) by Murakami Haruki, *Ningen Shikkaku* (Provalut na Choveka) by Dazai Osamu, *Haru no Yuki* (Proleten Snyag) by Mishima Yukio, *Honba* (Galopirashti Kone) by Mishima Yukio, and *Hakase no Aishita Sūshiki* (Lyubimata Formula na Profesora) by Ogawa Yōko. Due to the Foundation's great support for Japanese literature promotion during the years, Bulgarian people have had the opportunity to further develop their image of and knowledge about Japan.

Another initiative of the Japan Foundation for strengthening the Japanese cultural presence in Bulgaria has been the provision of films and materials on Japan to the Japanese Embassy and other Bulgarian institutions, as part of its project "Overseas Japanese Film Festival" (*Kaigai Nihon Eigamatsuri*). For instance, in the 2000s and the 2010s, programs related to Japan have been broadcasted on the Bulgarian National Television (BNT). Such include "Japanese Traditional Culture", "Digital Book Guide to the Universe" "Hundred Views of the Fresh Nature", "Wonder Mathematics", "Hi-Tech Workers", "Sadako", "Children's Puppet Theater", "Japanese World Heritage", "Capital City, Tokyo 2005", and "Japanese People's Food Style". Programs presenting Japanese culture like "Japan's World Cultural Heritage – Sunlight Shrines, Castles and Heritages of the Ryūkyū Kingdom", "Searching National Treasure", and "Shirakami-Sanchi" were broadcasted on the BTV channel as well. In addition, the programs "Japan Out and About", "Knowledge Creating Company" and "Japan's Latest Technology" were presented by various other Bulgarian TV channels. The rich variety of Japanese films, provided thanks to the Japan Foundation's support, have contributed much to the construct of Bulgarian people's image and perceptions of Japanese culture and technological advancement.

Japanese-language education

The Japan Foundation has been actively contributing to Japanese language promotion in Bulgaria. For instance, since the 1980s, it has been implementing a program for dispatching short-term and long-term Japanese language and culture specialists to the Sofia University "St. Kliment Ohridski". Until 2018, more than ten Japanese language experts and four assistants have been dispatched through the program. From the 1980s, the Foundation has also been conducting consultation sessions and training programs for non-native Japanese language teachers of various educational institutions in Bulgaria, enabling them to improve both their Japanese language skills and their teaching methodology. In addition, since the 2000s, it has been holding symposiums and seminars on Japanese language studies in Bulgaria. A case in point are the symposiums held between 2005 and 2010, focused on enhancing Japanese language education standards in Bulgaria and in neighboring countries, as well as on nurturing the information exchange and networks among the Japanese language teachers in the area.

As part of its cultural initiatives in Bulgaria, the Japan Foundation has been implementing a variety of Japanese language training programs. For example, since the 1980s, it has been holding a training in Japan for Bulgarian students with excellent performance in their Japanese language studies. The training's objectives are to encourage Japanese language learning in Bulgaria and to promote cultural exchange and mutual understanding through various activities such as lectures and university visits, trips within Japan, and homestay in Japanese houses. The program also provides Bulgarian students with the opportunity to experience Japanese culture and to establish relationships with Japanese people. In addition, from the 2000s, the Japan Foundation has been administering various other grant projects offering Japanese language trainings. For instance, it has been inviting Bulgarian university students and researchers who study Japanese at their faculty to Japan with the aim of deepening their skills and understanding of Japanese language, culture, and society through trainings, lectures, and exchange with Japanese university students. Until 2018, more than 18 Bulgarians have participated in the program. A specialized Japanese language training program for Bulgarian experts (*Senmon Nihongo Kenshū*), including civil servants, librarians, graduate students, and researchers, and a program for diplomats (*Gaikōkan Nihongo Kenshū*) have been held as well.

In addition to the aforementioned initiatives, to encourage Japanese language learning in Bulgaria, since the 2000s the Japan Foundation has been conducting a grant program for supporting Japanese language education at Bulgarian institutions and organizations (*Nihongo Fukyū Katsudou Josei*). Such institutions include the St. Cyril and St. Methodius International Foundation, the "Vasil Levski" High School in Ruse, the "Lyuben Karavelov" High School in Varna, the 138th "Prof. Vasil Zlatarski" High School in Sofia, the 40th "Louis Pasteur" High School in Sofia, the South-West University "Neofit Rilski", the Sofia University

"St. Kliment Ohridski", and the "St. Cyril and St. Methodius University" of Veliko Tarnovo. Since the 1970s, the Japan Foundation has also been donating Japanese language teaching materials to the Sofia University "St. Kliment Ohridski".

As part of its public diplomacy initiatives for Japanese language promotion in Bulgaria, the Japan Foundation has been subsidizing the implementation of the Japanese-Language Proficiency Test in the country, held in cooperation with the Japanese Embassy and the St. Cyril and St. Methodius International Foundation. In addition, it has been supporting the organization of the Japanese Language Speech Contest in Bulgaria. Initiated in 1994, the event is conducted annually in collaboration with the Japanese Embassy and the St. Cyril and St. Methodius International Foundation. The prize for first place at the Advanced Level – a trip to Japan – motivates the contestants to achieve high Japanese language skills and provides them with the opportunity to experience Japanese culture.

Japanese studies and intellectual exchange

The Japan Foundation has been exercising a variety of public diplomacy initiatives both autonomously and together with other public diplomacy actors to promote Japanese studies and intellectual exchange in Bulgaria. The grant program for supporting international collaborative research projects is a case in point. Since the 1990s, the Foundation has been providing subsidies to conduct seminars, symposiums, and conferences on various topics in collaboration with Japanese and Bulgarian institutions. For instance, in 2018 and 2019, together with the Sofia University "St. Kliment Ohridski", the Japan Foundation held an international conference entitled "Pop Culture and Youth in Japan and Bulgaria", focused on the relationship between Japan's pop culture and the social behavior of the young people as well as on the reception of the Japanese pop culture in Bulgaria.

To develop specialists on Japan in Bulgaria and to strengthen the Japanese research network, since 1978 the Japan Foundation has been implementing the Japanese Studies Fellowship Program, offering research fellowships to Japanese studies scholars in diverse fields. For instance, between 2001 and 2017, the following research projects have been carried out in Japan through the program – the "Functional and Aesthetical Consideration in the Design of the Urban Environment", the "Japanese Ethnography Textbook: Introductory Texts on Japanese Culture, Folklore, Philosophy and Way of Life for Students", the "Digging Out the Embedded Cultural Realities: Fairy Tales of Japan", the "Japanese Phonetics in Bulgarian", the "History of Soviet-Japanese Relations 1945–1960", and others. The initiative has been providing Bulgarian scholars with the opportunity not only to conduct research at Japanese universities, but also to experience Japanese culture and establish various relationships. In addition, apart from the Fellowship Program, since the 1990s the Foundation has been administering invitation programs for Bulgarian experts, scholars, teachers, and special guests.

To promote Japanese studies and culture in Bulgaria, the Japan Foundation has been donating a variety of books on Japan to Bulgarian institutions. In the 1970s, such institutions included the Sofia University "St. Kliment Ohridski" and the "St. St. Cyril and Methodius" National Library. In the 1980s, books were also provided to the Central Library of the Bulgarian Academy of Sciences. In the following years, the number of institutions expanded to include the Plovdiv University "Paisii Hilendarski", the "St. Cyril and St. Methodius University" of Veliko Tarnovo, and the University of National and World Economy.

Comparison and space for improvement of the Japan Foundation's performance in France and Bulgaria

Comparison

As was already demonstrated, the Japan Foundation has been greatly contributing to Japan's cultural promotion in France and Bulgaria. Since the beginning of its initiatives in the two countries, it has been active in all the three sections – art and cultural exchange, Japanese-language education, and Japanese studies and intellectual exchange. The Foundation has been conducting a rich variety of activities presenting aspects of Japanese traditional and contemporary culture. Crucial for the successful organization and implementation of those projects have been both its systematic efforts and its cooperation with various public and private actors. In Bulgaria, such actors have been the Embassy of Japan in Sofia, Bulgarian institutions like the St. Cyril and St. Methodius International Foundation, the Sofia University "St. Kliment Ohridski", friendship associations like the Fukuyama Bulgaria Association, and others. In France, the Foundation has been collaborating with essential Japanese actors including the Ministry of Foreign Affairs, the Embassy of Japan in Paris, JNTO, the Ministry of Economy, Trade and Industry, MAFF, MIC, JETRO, the Intellectual Property Strategy Promotion Bureau, the Agency for Cultural Affairs, the National Tax Agency, the Japan Tourism Agency, and others. From the French side, such actors have been MFAID, the French agency Campus France, the French film organization Cinematheque Francaise, various educational institutions like the Paris Diderot University, the College de France, the Lille 2 University of Health and Law, INALCO, and others. To promote Japanese culture in France, the Foundation has also been cooperating with crucial institutions like UNESCO and the European Association for Japanese Studies.

Following the previous discussion, it could be also emphasized that the Japan Foundation has been more active in its cultural promotion initiatives in France than in Bulgaria. First, there is a big difference in the number of the Foundation's projects carried out in the two countries. According to the full list of activities provided by the Japan Foundation, 4618 projects were conducted in France between April 1973 and April 2018, while in Bulgaria 676 projects were implemented between August 1974 and July 2018.[4] Second, the variety of projects in France has been much greater. For instance, in the field of art and cultural exchange, the Foundation's initiatives in Bulgaria have been presenting mostly aspects of Japanese traditional culture, while activities demonstrating Japanese contemporary culture have been considerably fewer. At the same time, there have been more projects presenting Japanese modern culture in France such as the special program for promoting the understanding of Japanese contemporary culture (*Gendaini-hon Rikai Tokubetsu Puroguramu*). In terms of the Japan Foundation's initiatives for introducing Japanese traditional culture, again, the projects in France have been more diverse than have those in Bulgaria. In addition, to further strengthen its activities and cultural exchange with France, the Foundation has also been conducting surveys at French organizations and various discussions.

A crucial factor for the greater number and diversity of projects presenting both traditional and contemporary Japanese culture in France has been the Japan Foundation's Japan Cultural Institute in Paris. Since its establishment in 1997, the number of Japan's public diplomacy initiatives increased in France. It has been implementing and co-sponsoring a variety of Japanese cultural activities in the country both autonomously and in collaboration with Japanese and French public diplomacy actors. As was demonstrated in the prior discussion, in the sphere of art and cultural exchange such projects included exhibitions, performances of theater and Japanese traditional and contemporary music, lectures, meetings, symposiums and demonstrations of Japanese arts, and many others. In the field of Japanese language education, the Institute has also been offering Japanese language courses and hosting Japanese language education guidance and workshops. Similarly, in the sphere of Japanese studies and intellectual exchange, with the contribution of the Institute, a higher number and greater variety of the Foundation's activities have been conducted in France than in Bulgaria.

As was observed in this study, taking into account the case of France as well as other European countries with established Japanese cultural institutes, the Japan Foundation's cultural promotion activity in Europe has been

focused to a great extent on the Western countries. This tendency was probably initiated as a result of the international situation and Japan's foreign
relations and priorities at the time when the Foundation was created. The
Japan Foundation was established in 1972 with the aim of improving its
relations with the United States and the promotion of cultural exchanges
between the two countries (Kokusaikōryūkikin 30-nen hensan-shitsu,
2006, pp. 20–21). At the same time, in light of Japan's economic growth
and its increasing international role, cultural exchanges and cultural diplomacy have become a great priority for Japan. In addition, in the 1970s, the
Foundation's purpose was also to strengthen Japan's relations and cultural
activities in Southeast Asia in response to the rise of anti-Japanese sentiments on the continent (Ogoura, 2009, p. 47). At the time, Europe was
considered Japan's essential economic partner, and the cultural cooperation and exchanges conducted through the Japan Foundation were of much
importance. Moreover, during the Cold War there were more opportunities
for Japanese cultural promotion in Western Europe than in Eastern Europe.
Japan and the Western European countries were both members of the Western Bloc, which provided a favorable environment and more space for such
cultural initiatives, while the regime in the East European countries had
led to certain limitations. As a result, although the Japan Foundation has
been carrying out cultural projects in both Western and Eastern Europe,
it tended to put more emphasis on its public diplomacy in the West. Such
evidence has been the establishment of its cultural institutes. After the Cold
War ended in 1993, the Japan Foundation increased its policies for cultural exchanges with Eastern Europe with the aim of promoting cooperation
and supporting democratization and openness of the countries in the region
(Kokusaikōryūkikin 30-nen hensan-shitsu, 2006, pp. 74–75).

Space for improvement

As was emphasized earlier, the Japan Cultural Institute in Paris has been
offering broad opportunities to the French public to explore Japanese culture, through either organizing or serving as a venue for the conduct of various projects. However, in order to further strengthen Japan's soft power in
France, the Japan Foundation should carry out more activities in various
French cities, rather than focusing mainly on Paris. As the scholar Michel
Wasserman highlighted during his personal communication with the author
of this study, it is necessary to "increase Japan's presence outside Paris"
(personal communication, April 12, 2019). Wasserman (personal communication, April 12, 2019) also emphasized, "France has cultural institutes in
many Japanese provincial cities, which is not the case of Japan in France".
To achieve a higher cultural presence in the country, the Japan Foundation

should establish additional branches of the Japan Cultural Institute in various French cities as well as cooperate with local institutions for the conduct of Japanese cultural initiatives. In this way, it will reach a greater number of people and provide them with the opportunity to extend their knowledge of and interest in Japan.

In the case of Bulgaria, there is still space for improvement of the Japan Foundation's initiatives in the country. First, besides the two-day annual festival "Aniventure", there are few opportunities for the Bulgarian public to become acquainted with and experience Japanese contemporary culture. However, the Bulgarian people's interest in Japan's modern culture has tended to grow over the years. Such evidence is the increasing number of visitors at the "Aniventure" festival. For instance, in 2008 the number of the guests was 700, in 2009 it was 1000, followed by 4000 people in 2013 and 20,000 people in 2017 (Aniventure, 2019). Therefore, in order to further increase Japan's cultural presence in Bulgaria, the Foundation should organize a greater number of activities and events featuring aspects of Japanese contemporary culture. Second, apart from the "Days of Japanese Culture" held by the Japanese Embassy with the support of the Japan Foundation and other actors, additional events introducing Japanese culture in Bulgaria throughout the year have been relatively few. This is to some extent due to the lack of a particular institution like the Japan Cultural Institute in Paris, which would regularly organize or host such activities. Third, the Japan Foundation does not offer Japanese language courses and workshops in Bulgaria as it does at the Japan Cultural Institute in Paris. However, Bulgarians' interest in studying Japanese language tends to be growing. According to the Embassy of Japan in Bulgaria, the number of Japanese language learners has considerably increased in the last three years, exceeding 1400 people (Embassy of Japan in Bulgaria, n.d.). Therefore, it would be valuable if the Foundation would establish more opportunities for studying Japanese language in the country. Taking into account the aforementioned issues, to further strengthen Japan's public diplomacy initiatives in Bulgaria it is crucial to create the Japan Foundation's Japan Cultural Institute or a similar institution in the country. As the scholar Bratislav Ivanov also highlighted during his personal communication with the author of this study, to achieve a higher Japanese cultural presence in the country "the establishment of a Japanese cultural center like China's Confucius Institute would be very good" (personal communication, February 17, 2019).

The creation of a Japanese cultural institute in Bulgaria would greatly enhance Japanese public diplomacy in Europe. First, the Japan Foundation has some offices and cultural institutes in Western or Central European countries, but none in Eastern Europe. In addition, as part of a global initiative of the Japanese Ministry of Foreign Affairs, a Japan House presenting

Japanese art, design, gastronomy, innovation, and technology opened in 2018 in London (Japan House, 2019). In this way, Japan's cultural activities have been implemented mostly in Western or Central Europe. Therefore, the foundation of an institute in Bulgaria could serve as a platform for promoting Japanese culture not only in the country, but also in Eastern Europe.

This first institute in the region would attract visitors from various countries to experience Japanese culture and could also serve as an example and a framework for the establishment of similar institutions in Eastern Europe. Second, it could be utilized by the Japan Foundation as a hub and a venue for the conduct of various initiatives either autonomously or in collaboration with other public and private actors. Third, the Institute would compensate for the insufficient or missing points of the Foundation's activities in Bulgaria and provide Bulgarians with a wide range of opportunities for extending their knowledge about Japan. For example, there could be regular courses and cultural activities dedicated to both Japanese language and culture. Such might include workshops and demonstrations of *ikebana* flower arrangement, *manga* comic books, tea ceremony, *go* game, calligraphy, *origami* paper folding, Japanese food, Japanese traditional dances, and others. In addition, the systematically organized initiatives of the Institute would provide the Bulgarian public with the chance to experience Japanese culture throughout the year. Through the Institute, the Foundation could conduct and host various activities in the fields of visual and performing arts, including exhibitions, music, and dance performances, as well as conferences, seminars, and lectures, introducing aspects of both traditional and contemporary Japanese culture. At the same time, the invited guests from all backgrounds would further contribute to the intellectual exchange, creativity, and mutual understanding between the Bulgarian and Japanese society. As Japan's Prime Minister Shinzo Abe emphasized at the summit meeting with the Bulgarian Prime Minister Boyko Borisov during his visit in Bulgaria in 2018, Japan hopes "to promote further exchange with Bulgaria, including the expansion of people-to-people exchanges" (Ministry of Foreign Affairs of Japan, 2018). In parallel with the cooperation in the field of culture, both leaders expressed their desire for the further development of the bilateral economic and political relations. Another essential role of the institute would be the provision of books on Japan and the regular projection of Japanese feature films and animations. According to Bratislav Ivanov (personal communication, February 17, 2019), "unfortunately, original Japanese books cannot be purchased in Bulgaria, and those accessible in the libraries are few and, in most cases, outdated".

After the Cold War, there has been a greater variety of activities introducing Japanese culture in Eastern Europe. However, as was indicated in this study, despite past and current efforts, there is still much space for improvement. In order to increase its soft power on the continent, it is crucial for Japan to put more emphasis on its public diplomacy in Eastern Europe. Taking into account the Economic Partnership Agreement (EPA) between Japan and the European Union entered into force on February 1, 2019, which provides new trade and investment opportunities, Japanese public diplomacy would become even more essential and contributory to the increase of the positive image of Japan and its relations with Europe. Therefore, similar to the cases in Western Europe, the establishment of the Japan Foundation's cultural institutes or analogous institutions in Bulgaria and other East European countries would be vital. This would compensate for the scarceness of Japanese cultural presence in the region and provide more opportunities for international cooperation. At the same time, to further expand the Foundation's activity and networks in France, the creation of more branches of the Japan Cultural Institute in various French cities would be also significant. Utilized as hubs for the conduct of Japanese cultural promotion initiatives in Europe, the institutes could regularly exercise various projects and facilitate cooperation among the Japan Foundation and other Japanese and European public and private actors on the continent.

Notes

1 The society was founded in 1822 by Antoine Isaac Silvestre de Sacy (1758–1838) and Abel-Rémusat, who were considered eminent representatives of Oriental studies at the time (Belouad, 2014, p. 218).
2 Currently known as the National Institute for Oriental Languages and Civilizations (INALCO).
3 These works included *Japan Notes* by Milan Milanov (Yaponski belejnik, 1972), *Japan: Contemporary Issues* by Todor Petkov (Yaponiya: suvremenni problemi i dilemata, 1975), *Japan as It Is* by Marko Semov (Yaponiya kato za Yaponiya, 1984), *Zen Aesthetics and the Japanese Art Tradition* by Boyka Tsigova (Dzen estetikata i yaponskata hudojestvena traditsiya, 1988), *The Art of Ikebana* by Rima Mirska (Izkustvoto ikebana, 1988), *Japan: From Katana to Artificial Intellect* by Nacho Papazov (Yaponiya: ot samuraiskiya mech do izkustveniya intelekt, 1989), and *Following the Brush* by Tsvetana Krasteva (Po sledite na chetkata, 1994).
4 The Japan Foundation projects for Bulgaria in the period between 1973 and 2018 and the Japan Foundation projects for France in the period between 1973 and 2018 (Unpublished documents). The documents were kindly provided to the author of the present study by the Japan Foundation.

References

Aniventure. (2019). *Za Aniventure* [About Aniventure]. Retrieved August 21, 2019, from https://aniventure.net/bg/info/about-aniventure

Belouad, C. (2014). Léon de Rosny, pioneer des études japonaises en France, et ses activités de présentation de la littérature et de la culture japonaises [Leon de Rosny, pioneer of Japanese studies in France, and his activities of presentation of Japanese literature and culture]. In Y. Ishige, T. Kashiwagi, & N. Kobayashi (Eds.), *Les échanges culturels entre le Japon et la France: autour de la collection japonaise d'Emmanuel Tronquois* [Cultural exchanges between Japan and France: Around the Japanese collection of Emmanuel Tronquois] (pp. 215–242). Kyoto: Shibunkaku shuppan.

Embassy of Japan in Bulgaria. (n.d.). Obshta Informatsia [General information]. *Dvustranni otnosheniya* [Bilateral relations]. Retrieved November 19, 2017, from www.bg.emb-japan.go.jp/itpr_bg/bg_jap_relations.html

Encyclopedia of Art History. (n.d.). Japonism. *Encyclopedia of Art History*. Retrieved January 29, 2019, from www.visual-arts-cork.com/history-of-art/japonism.htm

Japan House. (n.d.). *What is Japan house?* Retrieved August 24, 2019, from www.japanhouselondon.uk/about/what-is-japan-house/

Japonismes 2018. (2018). *Japonismes 2018 – Framework*. Retrieved from https://japonismes.org/wp-content/uploads/2018/04/framework.pdf

Kandilarov, E. (2012). Lyudmila Zhivkova i kulturnata diplomatsiya kum Yaponiya [Lyudmila Zhivkova and the cultural diplomacy towards Japan]. *Novo Vreme, 11*, 89–102.

Kandilarov, E. (2016). *Iztochna Azia I Bulgaria* [East Asia and Bulgaria]. Sofia: Iztok-Zapad.

Kokusaikōryūkikin 30-nen hensan-shitsu [The editing room for the history of the Japan foundation in the past 30 years]. (2006). *Kokusaikōryūkikin 30-nen no Ayumi* [The history of the Japan Foundation in the past 30 years]. Tokyo: The Japan Foundation.

Lacambre, G. (1983). Japonisme [Japanism]. In *Les Arts décoratifs (France)* [Decorative arts (France)], *France. Délégation aux arts plastiques* [France. Delegation of plastic arts], *Musée des arts décoratifs (Paris)* [Museum of decorative arts], *Le Livre des expositions universelles, 1851–1989 : [exposition, Paris, Musée des arts décoratifs, juin-12 décembre 1983]/[organisée par l'Union centrale des arts décoratifs]; [avec le concours du Ministère de la culture, Délégation aux arts plastiques]* [The book of world expositions, 1851–1989: [exposition, Paris, Museum of Decorative Arts, June – December 12, 1983]/organized by the Central Union of Decorative Arts]; [with the assistance of the Ministry of Culture, Delegation of Plastic Arts] (pp. 297–304). Paris: Éditions des arts décoratifs [Decorative arts editions] and Paris: Herscher.

Maison de la culture du Japon à Paris. (2019). *La MCJP en quelques mots* [The MCJP in a few words]. Retrieved January 31, 2019, from www.mcjp.fr/fr/la-mcjp/presentation

Ministry of Foreign Affairs of Japan. (2018, January 14). *Japan-Bulgaria Relations: Japan-Bulgaria expanded summit meeting and summit dinner meeting*. Retrieved from www.mofa.go.jp/erp/c_see/bg/page1e_000200.html

Ministry of Foreign Affairs of Japan. (2019). *Diplomatic Bluebook 2019: Japan's foreign policy to promote national and global interests.* Retrieved from www. mofa.go.jp/policy/other/bluebook/2019/html/chapter3/c030402.html

Ministry of Foreign Affairs of Japan. (2020, August 27). *Japan-France relations (basic data).* Retrieved January 31, 2019, from www.mofa.go.jp/region/europe/france/data.html

Ogoura, K. (2009). *Japan's Cultural Diplomacy, Past and Present.* Joint Research Institute for International Peace and Culture. Tokyo: Aoyama Gakuin University, 44–54.

Petkova, G. (2012). Promotion and reception of Japanese culture in Bulgaria. *Seijo CJS Reports*, no. 1. Tokyo: Center for Glocal Studies, Seijo University.

Vutova-Stefanova, V. (2016). BULARIYA-YAPONIYA, Dialog i obmen mejdu dve kulturi [BULGARIA-JAPAN, Dialogue and exchange between two cultures]. In Gergana P., Andreev A., Koleva E., Todorova A. (Eds.), *Japan – Times, Spirituality and Perspectives* (pp. 137–169). Sofia: Universitetsko izdatelstvo "Sv. Kliment Ohridski".

Watanabe, H. (2018). The 160th anniversary of Franco-Japanese diplomatic relations: How France discovered Japonisme. *Discuss Japan, Japan Foreign Policy Forum, Ministry of Foreign Affairs of Japan, Diplomacy*, 49. Retrieved from www.japanpolicyforum.jp/pdf/2018/no49/DJweb_49_dip_03.pdf

5 A framework of an integrated public diplomacy in Europe

The Japan Foundation as a major public diplomacy actor

Potential and limitations of the Japan Foundation

The already established networks for collaboration with a variety of public and private actors in France and Bulgaria highlighted in this study, as well as the Japan Foundation's special role in the conduct of the Japonismes 2018 event, demonstrated its strong potential for becoming Japan's major public diplomacy actor in Europe. The Foundation was chosen by the Japanese government to be responsible for the planning and implementation of the project as a secretariat for Japonismes 2018, coordinating the conducted initiatives in cooperation with the involved French and Japanese institutions. Thanks to the well-organized initiatives and the tight collaboration among the Japan Foundation and the other public and private actors, the event ended with great success. As Japanese Foreign Press Secretary Takeshi Osuga highlights, Japonismes 2018 was "this century's largest overseas project for introducing Japanese culture", attended by "over three million people, a number which far exceeds the population of Paris" (Ministry of Foreign Affairs of Japan, 2019). The project was also highly beneficial for the increase of the interest in Japan from the French side. A questionnaire filled out by about 10,000 people revealed that 86% of the interviewees "began to feel that they want to learn more about Japan", and 96% responded that they "began to feel a larger affinity with Japan" (Ministry of Foreign Affairs of Japan, 2019).

Together with the Japan Foundation's contribution to the promotion of Japanese culture in Europe and its earlier emphasized role, other factors also reveal its potential for becoming Japan's major public diplomacy actor on the continent. First, historically the Japan Foundation has been Japan's first institution established with the aim of introducing Japanese culture abroad. It facilitates the broadest network for cooperation with various Japanese and local public and private actors in Europe and worldwide. Second, during Japan's Central Government Reform in 2001, the

DOI: 10.4324/9781003006251-5

functions related to the promotion of cultural exchange became divided between the Ministry of Foreign Affairs, the Agency for Cultural Affairs, and the Japan Foundation. Following the reform, the Japan Foundation and the Ministry of Foreign Affairs' cultural exchange activity became limited to diplomacy (Kaneko & Kitano, 2014, p. 215). This decision demonstrated the leading role of the Foundation as Japan's public diplomacy actor. Third, while the Japanese Embassy has been implementing a variety of cultural initiatives, it has certain limitations in comparison with the Japan Foundation. Together with the strengthening of the cultural relations between Japan and the European countries, the embassy has other missions and responsibilities in various fields. This provides fewer opportunities to focus on Japan's cultural promotion, which, on the other hand, has been the Japan Foundation's major task. Fourth, through its initiatives for introducing Japanese culture, language, studies, and intellectual exchange programs, the Foundation plays a crucial role in the nurturing of the interest towards Japan in Europe in a long-term perspective. Finally, an outstanding feature of the Foundation is also the broad type of audience that it reaches, ranging from the younger generation to the elite, the middle-aged, and the senior generation, due to the variety of cultural spheres that it covers.

At the same time, some points are necessary to be addressed for the Japan Foundation to reach its full potential for becoming Japan's major public diplomacy actor in Europe. First, as was emphasized previously, there are no offices of the Foundation in the East European countries. The establishment of the Foundation's cultural institutes is essential for coordinating its activities to a greater extent, for implementing a richer variety of projects that introduce Japanese culture on a regular basis, and for achieving a higher cultural presence on the continent. Second, although the functions of the Agency for Cultural Affairs and the Japan Foundation became divided after the Japan's Central Government Reform in 2001, they have been still overlapping in certain initiatives. The two institutions should collaborate on the clear separation of their activity as well as on the coordination of the projects' content in order to enhance their efficiency, introduce Japanese cultural aspects to a broader extent, and economize funds spent on similar activities. Third, while the Japan Foundation strictly provides information regarding its finances, the description of its projects' efficacy has been insufficient. As Kaneko and Kitano (2014, p. 217) highlight, the Foundation is required to more clearly explain the effectiveness of its initiatives. The creation of a system evaluating the efficiency of the implemented projects would be crucial for strengthening the potential of the Foundation as Japan's main public diplomacy actor facilitating a platform for public and private partnerships.

Finally, as already emphasized, a major issue of Japan's public diplomacy has been the lack of integration among the actors from the public and private sectors and the insufficient collaboration among them. In addition, Japan's budget and activities related to public diplomacy have been limited and need to be expanded (Kaneko & Kitano, 2014, p. 225). As Kaneko and Kitano (2014, p. 225) point out, Japanese actors like the Ministry of Foreign Affairs, government offices, ministries, and government agencies should work together to strengthen the mutual cooperation and the public-private partnerships in order to achieve higher effects with the limited resources. There should be a mechanism for sharing information on international exchange programs conducted by the various ministries and the private sector as well as for coordinating their projects (Kaneko & Kitano, 2014, p. 225). Therefore, in order to serve as a central public diplomacy actor of Japan in Europe, together with its collaboration with the Ministry of Foreign Affairs and the other current partners, the Japan Foundation should expand its network and further cooperate with additional institutions promoting Japanese culture. The Foundation's cultural institutes could be utilized as hubs for the conduct and the coordination of the integrated initiatives of such institutions and the Foundation. This Public-Private Partnership Platform would strengthen the collaborations between the public and private sectors and further increase Japanese cultural presence on the continent.

In order to provide a framework of suggestions concerning Japan's integrated public diplomacy in Europe, it is essential to examine other cultural promotion actors that have been collaborating with the Japan Foundation or have a potential for future cooperation through the Public-Private Partnership Platform. In addition, for the construction of more efficient project proposals for Japan's future initiatives, it is crucial to explore the European expectations from Japan and the insufficient points and less explored areas in terms of its soft power on the continent. These issues are going to be addressed in the following subchapters through the cases of France and Bulgaria.

Prospective partners of the Japan Foundation in France and Bulgaria

In the case of France

Together with the Japan Foundation, crucial Japanese public diplomacy actors in France have been the Ministry of Foreign Affairs of Japan and the Japanese Embassy. They have been cooperating with the Japan Foundation and its Japan Cultural Institute in Paris as well as with French and Japanese public and private institutions on the organization of initiatives and events promoting Japanese culture. One such example is the aforementioned Japonismes 2018 project.

The Japanese government's Cabinet Office in collaboration with various public and private actors such as the Ministry of Economy, Trade and Industry of Japan has also been an essential public diplomacy actor in France. In line with its Cool Japan Strategy, it has been conducting a variety of initiatives and events to promote Japanese contemporary and traditional culture in the country. One such example is the "DISCOVER KANSAI Project" in Paris between November 2017 and January 2018, organized by the Kinki Bureau of Economy, Trade and Industry in cooperation with the regional Ministry of Economy, Trade and Industry, the Paris showroom management company SAS ENIS, JETRO, and other organizations in charge of Cool Japan related activities. The project focused on reexamining and strengthening Japan's business framework as a new "Challenge Local Cool Japan in Paris" project, aimed at the creation of new markets for industry (Kinki Bureau of Economy, Trade and Industry, 2018). The initiative consisted of an exhibition of 34 Japanese products at the Maison Wa in Paris.

Another example of the Cabinet Office's public diplomacy activity, conducted as part of its Cool Japan Initiative, is the "Japanese Food Culture Promotion Project" held in France between September 2012 and March 2013. During the event, there was a "Japanese Culinary Culture Fair 2012" – a workshop by Japanese cooks targeted at the French wealthy class, "Japan Table Art Exhibition" – an exhibition and sale of tableware products at large department stores, and collaborations with French-cuisine restaurants for offering Japanese food in those restaurants' menu (Ministry of Economy, Trade and Industry, n.d.). The project was organized in cooperation with French and Japanese partners such as the *Chambre de Commerce et d'Industrie Française du Japon* (French Chamber of Commerce and Industry of Japan), HAKUHODO Inc., Isetan Mitsukoshi Holdings Ltd., Galeries Lafayette, *Chambre de Commerce et d'Industrie de Paris* (Paris Chamber of Commerce and Industry), and others.

Together with the aforementioned crucial institutions, Japanese culture and language have been introduced through a variety of other public diplomacy actors in France, greatly contributing to the strengthening of Japan's cultural presence in France. Starting from Rosny's activities in the 19th century for promoting Japanese language and studies in France, in the 20th and 21st centuries the number of institutions offering Japanese language studies has much increased in the country. As the Ministry of Foreign Affairs of Japan (2020) highlights, "with the popularity of pop culture, Japanese language learners are also increasing (about 24,000 people in 2018)". This achievement is to a great extent due to the rich palette of public diplomacy initiatives for Japanese cultural promotion implemented in the country.

In France, Japanese has been taught in primary schools, high schools, and colleges in many major cities like Paris, Bordeaux, Caen, Lille, Lyon, Nantes, Nice, Reims, Rennes, Strasbourg, Toulouse, and others. There are also various universities in the country offering Japanese language and studies courses. These include the Aix-Marseille University (Japanese studies section), the Bordeaux Montaigne University (Japanese studies section), the Grenoble Alpes University (subsection of Japanese language), the Jean Moulin University Lyon III (department of Japanese studies), the University of Nantes (section of Japanese language), the French National Institute for Oriental Languages and Civilizations (INALCO) (departments of Japanese studies), the IGR-IAE Rennes Graduate School of Management (courses on Japanese companies management), the University of Strasbourg (department of Japanese studies), the University of Toulouse-Jean Jaurès (section of Japanese language), and a few others in Paris, Versailles, Rouen, Lille, and Orleans Tours. Together with the rich variety of institutions offering Japanese language and studies in France, academic exchange between France and Japan has also been increasing (Ministry of Foreign Affairs of Japan, 2020). According to the Ministry of Foreign Affairs of Japan (2020), there are about 1,000 France-Japan inter-university agreements at present, implementing programs in the field of student exchange. Such examples are the French universities Sciences Po Rennes, PSB Paris School of Business, Toulouse Business School, and others offering study abroad programs in partner institutions in Japan. In addition, a Japanese organization contributing much to the promotion of student exchanges between France and Japan has been the Japan Student Services Organization (JASSO). It provides information on studying in Japan and financial assistance for French and other international students, as well as develops programs to promote exchange among international students. Thanks to such inter-university agreements and organizations' programs, French students have been able to experience Japanese culture and establish relationships, while extending their knowledge and skills in various academic disciplines at universities in Japan.

Another Japanese institution playing a significant role in the field of education and exchange has been the Japan Society for the Promotion of Science (JSPS). Supported mainly by annual subsides from the Japanese government, JSPS aims "to foster young researchers", "to promote international scientific cooperation", "to award Grants-in-Aid for Scientific Research", "to support scientific cooperation between the academic community and industry", and "to collect and distribute information on scientific research activities" (Japan Society for the Promotion of Science, n.d.). In 2001, it established a JSPS Strasbourg Office in France, through which it implements a variety of initiatives like university visits, conferences, and organization of forums in the country. It also conducts bilateral programs with

French organizations like CNRS, l'INRA, l'INSERM, l'INRIA, l'ANR, l'IHÉS, MAEE, and MESR (JSPS Strasbourg office, n.d.). In addition, the JSPS Strasbourg Office offers the JSPS Postdoctoral Fellowship Program, enabling French researchers to carry out joint research activities in Japan.

To project an image of itself as a technologically advanced nation, Japan has been implementing diverse initiatives the field of science and technology in France. A crucial institution in this sphere is the Japan Science and Technology Agency (JST). It aims to "establish Japan as a nation built on the creativity of science and technology, as a core organization for implementing Japan's science and technology policy in line with the objectives of the Science and Technology Basic Plan" (Japan Science and Technology Agency France, PARIS Office, n.d.). In 1984 JST established the JST Paris Office, which is used as contact point in Europe for JST and for Japanese science and technology. The office is in charge of various initiatives in France and other European countries. For instance, it "provides support for the overseas extension of JST programs, collects and disseminates the latest information on science and technology in Europe, and engages in other such activities that advance Japanese science and technology as well as strengthen its presence" (Japan Science and Technology Agency France, PARIS Office, n.d.).

In the 20th and 21st centuries, not only the interest in Japanese language and studies, but also the appreciation of Japanese literature was maintained in France, leading to the issue of a great number of books and publications on Japan and Japonism. Some examples include *Le Japon illustré* (Japan Illustrated) by Félicien Challaye in 1915, *Sèvres: Les débuts du japonisme céramique en France* (Sèvres: The Beginnings of Ceramic Japonism in France) by Laurens d'Albis in 1998, *Henri Rivière: Entre impressionnisme et japonisme* (Henri Rivière: Between Impressionism and Japonism) by Valérie Sueur-Hermel in 2009, *Japonismes* by Olivier Gabet in 2014, *Les Échanges culturels entre le Japon et la France: Autour de la collection japonaise d'Emmanuel Tronquois* (Cultural Exchanges between Japan and France: Around the Japanese Collection of Emmanuel Tronquois) by Yumi Ishige in 2014, *Au coeur du Japon* (In the Heart of Japan) by Laurent Martein in 2018, and thousands of others. In addition, to strengthen its cultural presence in the field of literature, Japan has been participating in book exhibitions in France. For instance, in 2012, Japan was the honorary guest country at the "Salon du Livre" book exhibition in Paris, where 20 Japanese writers were invited and took part in lecture events (Ministry of Foreign Affairs of Japan, 2020).

Various institutes and associations in France have also been offering online journals with articles and information on Japan. *Cipango – French Journal of Japanese Studies* is a case in point. It is facilitated by the Centre for Japanese Studies of INALCO. Established in 2012, Cipango publishes articles in both French and English. Another example of an association offering online journals in France is Jipango, a Japanese cultural association, which between 1998 and 2011 has issued a variety of articles on Japan. Currently, it is focused on conducting activities introducing Japanese culture. In addition to the associations and institutes, online magazines and social media in France have been offering news and information on Japan. One such example is the *Japon infos* magazine, facilitated by the agency JAPON INFORMATION SAS, a Franco-Japanese company for consulting, communication, and media. Another magazine on Japan in France is *ZOOM Japon*, published by Editions Ilyfunet. It offers news and information related to Japanese politics, economy, and culture. The magazine presents major Japanese events in France as well as emphasizes Japanese cuisine and tourism in Japan (ZOOM Japon, n.d.).

In the 20th and 21st centuries, Japanese arts have been promoted in France through a great variety of actors. For instance, tea ceremony courses have been available at the Urasenke Tankokai Seiryu, the Tea School, and the Japan Foundation's Japan Cultural Institute in Paris. There have also been associations in France offering *ikebana* flower arrangement lessons. Some examples include the association atelier Mizuki de Paris and the Ikebana Sogetsu Branche Française. In addition, *ikebana* flower arrangement courses have been conducted at the Japan Cultural Institute in Paris and the Franco-Japanese Floral Art Alliance (AFJAF). Japanese dances have also been taught at schools like the Ecole Human Dance and the NUBA Franco-Japanese dance company. Calligraphy courses have been offered at the Maison de la Calligraphie and the Association Calligraphis. A number of schools in the country also conduct Japanese martial arts lessons. These include the Taisho Dojo, the Ecole Traditionnelle D'Arts Martiaux Japonais (ETAMJ), the Ecoles Bushido, and the Tassin Ecole d'Arts Martiaux. Thanks to the rich palette of Japanese arts introduced in France, the French public has been able to broaden their image and knowledge of various aspects of Japanese culture.

Essential public diplomacy actors in France are the associations and foundations, promoting Japanese culture in the country. One such example established in 2014 is the Wakaba Association, which has been offering both Japanese language courses and lessons on *Yosakoi* dance, tea ceremony, calligraphy, *kitsuke* (kimono), *ikebana* flower arrangement, *taiko* drums, *origami* paper folding, *kendama* toy, Japanese cuisine, *manga* comic books, *kakemono* hanging scroll, and others. Every year in March, the association holds an event called "MATSURI". During the event, there is a concert of Japanese instruments like *taiko* and *shamisen* as well as festive music and

Bon-Odori dance. Japanese culture is also presented through demonstrations of martial arts, Japanese dishes, and Japanese cultural stands (Wakaba Association, 2019).

Highly contributory to the promotion of Japanese culture in France has been the Fondation Franco-Japonaise Sasakawa (Franco-Japanese Sasakawa Foundation). Established in 1990, it is a private, nonprofit organization with a French status. Its mission is to "develop cultural relations and friendship between France and Japan" (Fondation Franco-Japonaise Sasakawa, n.d.). The foundation is administered by a board of directors consisting of seven Japanese and eight French members who meet twice a year. The French minister of culture is also present or represented at the board. The foundation cooperates with various Japanese and French public and private actors, including the Japan Foundation's Japan Cultural Institute in Paris. It organizes both autonomously or in collaboration with its partners a variety of Japanese cultural projects in France such as exhibitions, concerts, *Kabuki* theater performances, and others.

During the 20th and 21st centuries, Japanese culture has also been introduced by the France-Japan friendship associations located in cities all over France. In June 2020, 171 associations have been registered, implementing "services aiming Japanese culture spread and Franco-Japanese cultural exchange" in the country (Ministry of Foreign Affairs of Japan, 2020). The friendship associations' main activities include the introduction of various Japanese cultural elements such as martial arts, calligraphy, tea ceremony, cooking lessons, exchanges, organization of events, *ikebana* flower arrangement, Japanese language courses, *origami* paper folding, and tutoring. There have also been other initiatives in the fields of architecture, lacquer art, *bonsai* tree, cinema, cosplay, dance, *haiku* poetry, karaoke, kimono, theatre, music, *taiko* drums, traditional games, and others. In addition, together with their regular activities, after the Great East Japan Earthquake in 2011, some France-Japan friendship associations held charity events and cultural exchanges.

Another essential institution exercising Japanese public diplomacy in France has been the Japan National Tourism Organization. It has an office in Paris and an official website in French through which it introduces Japanese arts, architecture, galleries, and museums as well as popular travel destinations in the country to encourage French people to visit Japan.

Starting from the 19th century, contributing greatly to the promotion of Japan's culture has been the rich palette of Japanese gardens in France. The gardens have been constructed in the regions of Auvergne-Rhone-Alps, Brittany, Grand Est, Hauts-de-France, Ile-de-France, Normandy, Occitanie, Pays de la Loire, Provence-Alpes-Cote d'Azur, and Monaco, displaying the serenity, creativity, and artistry of Japan to the French society. In addition, Japanese gardens have been conveying an image of Japan as a peaceful and harmonious country, which has been one of its public diplomacy strategies.

Since 1978, Japanese contemporary culture has also been widely promoted in France through various public diplomacy initiatives. One such example is the "Japan Expo", "probably the largest Japan culture event in the world" (Watanabe, 2018). Initiated in 1998, the event continues to be held every year, with a growing number of visitors. For instance, from 3200 attendees at the first edition, the number has reached 247,473 in 2015. Japan Expo offers a rich palette of initiatives organized both autonomously and in cooperation with public and private actors, including the Japan Foundation, the Ministry of Economy, Trade and Industry, and the Embassy of Japan in France. Its aim is to promote Japanese culture, "from *manga* to fashion, from animation to traditions and music and video games" (Japan Expo, 2018).

The Ministry of Foreign Affairs of Japan has also been conducting public diplomacy activities to introduce Japanese contemporary culture in France. One such example is the established in 2007 "International MANGA Award". The aim of the initiative is to expand "international exchange and mutual understanding through MANGA culture" (Ministry of Foreign Affairs of Japan, 2014a). The award honors *manga* artists, contributing to the promotion of *manga* comic books in various countries around the world including France. The committee consists of "the Minister for Foreign Affairs, the President of the Japan Foundation, and the members of the special committee for pop culture of the Council on the Movement of People Across Borders" (Ministry of Foreign Affairs of Japan, 2014b). The recipients of the award attend an award ceremony and are invited to Japan by the Japan Foundation for about ten days.

Japanese contemporary culture has been promoted through the variety of bookstores offering *manga* comic books around France. The Librairie japonaise Junku (Junku Japanese Bookstore), located in Paris, is a case in point. It sells not only Japanese comics and supplies for creating *manga*, but also Japanese literature, Japanese language textbooks, and Japan travel guidebooks, as well as goods and products from Japan like *origami* paper, calligraphy tools, and others. Apart from the Librairie japonaise Junku, there have been many stores in France where Japanese *manga*, animation, and *manga* figurines could be purchased. Such examples are Mangatori, KONCI, Asian Alternative, Manga Distribution, Manga Loisir, Mangarake, and Mangastore.

France is considered the second largest consumer of *manga* comic books in the world with more than 15 million copies sold in 2017 (Manga Café, 2018). In 2006, it was the first country to open a *manga* cafe in Europe – the

Manga Café V1. In 2011, a second cafe – Manga Café V2 – was established in Paris, and in 2013 the Manga Café V1 was closed. Located in Paris, the Manga Café V2 welcomes many *manga* fans every day. The visitors can enjoy reading more than 18,000 books, drink hot and cold drinks, and play arcade video games (Manga Café, 2018). They also have the opportunity to buy books, Japanese grocery and confectionery products, figurines, and Japanese meals.

Japanese cuisine has also been widely promoted in France. Since the 1960s, Japanese food began to be introduced in the country. It is considered that Japanese cooks who travelled to France served as "the beginnings of the development of a transition to Japanese-style food in French cuisine" (National Diet Library, Japan, n.d.). Since about the year 2000, Japanese food has become the "vogue in France, thanks to the Japanese sub-culture widely accepted by young generation and the adult/senior generations growing more and more health conscious" (Ministry of Economy, Trade and Industry, n.d.). Due to the growing popularity of Japanese cuisine in France, many restaurants and stores began to offer Japanese food as well as ingredients for its preparation. At the same time, various institutions such as the Cabinet Office, the Ministry of Economy, Trade and Industry, the Japan Foundation, and JETRO have been presenting Japanese cuisine in France. The initiatives have been focused not only on the introduction of Japanese food, but also on the development of human resources for Japanese cuisine in France. For instance, in 2016, as part of the "Human Resource Development for Japanese Cuisine/Food Culture" project implemented by the Ministry of Agriculture, Forestry and Fisheries of Japan, Le Cordon Bleu Japan offered a six-month fully funded culinary internship program for French culinary school graduates or industry professionals to learn culinary techniques from master chefs in Japan (Le Cordon Bleu, n.d.).

Due to the growing interest in Japanese contemporary culture, stores offering Cool Japan products have also been established in France. The Cool Japan boutique in Paris is a case in point. It sells a variety of genuine items, imported directly from Japan, such as traditional clothes, decorative objects, bowls, cups, *maneki neko* figurines, *daruma* dolls, and many others.

Apart from the aforementioned institutions, highly contributory public diplomacy actors for Japanese cultural promotion in France have been the Japanese nationals temporarily staying or living in the country. According to Masato Kitera (2018), former Japanese ambassador to France, there are more than 40,000 Japanese people living in France at present. In addition, in the field of Japanese studies, the number of Japanese language teachers has been growing (Kitera, 2018). Through the contacts and exchanges with Japanese representatives, French people have the opportunity to not only increase their knowledge and enrich their image of Japan, but also to establish valuable relationships contributing to the mutual understanding and relations between the two countries.

In the case of Bulgaria

Apart from the first Japanese cultural promotion activities in Bulgaria emphasized previously and the contribution of the Japan Foundation, there have been various other actors introducing Japanese culture in the country. From 1989, the Bulgarian transition from state socialism to a multiparty democracy provided many opportunities for Bulgarian-Japanese bilateral relations and public diplomacy initiatives. Since that time, Japanese cultural promotion in Bulgaria has been increasing to an even greater extent than before. Essential factors have been the "Japanese government's policy for presenting Japanese culture abroad, as well as the financial and organizational support of the Japan Foundation, the Japan International Cooperation Agency (JICA), and the Japan Overseas Cooperation Volunteers (JOCV) program" (Vera Vutova-Stefanova, personal communication, March 4, 2017).

From 1991, the governments of Japan and Bulgaria began exchanging letters in which they emphasized mutual cooperation on culture, science, education, and sport. An important initiative for strengthening this collaboration was the establishment of a program for student and scholar exchange between the Ministry of Education in Bulgaria and the Japan Society for the Promotion of Science as well as between the two countries' academic institutions – the Sofia University "St. Kliment Ohridski" and Soka University.

After the 1990s, Japanese language studies and literature achieved great development and popularity in Bulgaria. Many state and private institutions began to offer opportunities to the Bulgarian public for learning about Japan and its language and culture. One such institution was the Sofia University "St. Kliment Ohridski" which in 1990 initiated an M.A. program in Japanese studies. It was a five-year course during which students acquired skills in both Japanese language and Japanese studies. Following this, with the introduction of the European framework for development of higher education (also called the Bologna system), Sofia University was obliged to change the program into a four-year bachelor course which could be continued with an M.A. course in Asian Studies. As a result, new subjects such as sociology, international relations, ethnography, economy and management, and issues of contemporary Japan also became part of the curriculum (Petkova, 2012, p. 5). In 2000, the program turned into a separate unit of "Japanese Studies" within the Department of East Asian Languages and Cultures, and in 2018, the Department of Japanese Studies as an academic unit was created.

At present, the Sofia University "St. Kliment Ohridski" offers B.A., M.A., and Ph.D. degrees in Japanese Studies. It teaches a broad variety of academic subjects like Japanese art, philosophy, religion, theory and practice of Japanese language and literature, Japanese history, and traditional and contemporary culture. In addition, students and teaching staff engage in diverse events, as well as in national and international research projects. After graduation, students not only obtain excellent skills in Japanese language and a wide knowledge on Japan and its culture, but they also become a bridge between Japan and Bulgaria with their contribution to further Japanese cultural promotion.

Together with the B.A., M.A., and Ph.D. programs, Sofia University began offering a two-year open non-degree course held in the evening, which continues at present. The course consists of lessons on Japanese language and culture. Every year around 10–15 people enroll, varying from

> young specialists in various fields who wish to learn from the Japanese experience, middle-aged people who have a strong interest in Japan due to the intensive cultural exchange between the two countries, and fellows planning to go to Japan to study, work or do research or who have come back and wish to deepen their understanding and competency in Japanese language and culture.
>
> (Petkova, 2012, pp. 5–6)

Another contribution to the Japanese cultural promotion in Bulgaria by Sofia University is the research conducted by its seven-member full-time staff specialized in Japanese studies and language. The faculty publishes the results of their research, takes part in various academic activities, events, and international cooperation, as well as conducts projects with other specialists and students. For instance, in 2010 to commemorate its 20th anniversary the Japanese Studies Section held an international symposium, where "specialists from all around Bulgaria gathered to share their achievements in regard to the study and promotion of Japanese language and culture" (Petkova, 2012, p. 6).

The Department of Japanese Studies of the Sofia University "St. Kliment Ohridski" has successfully created a rich and stable basis for research and promotion of Japan and its culture in Bulgaria. This achievement is also to a great extent due to the collaboration and support provided by the Japan Foundation, which each year sends Japanese language specialists and a variety of literature to Sofia University's library. For instance, currently there are more than 5000 volumes on Japan at the library of the Sofia University's Centre for Eastern Languages and Cultures (Petkova, 2012, p. 6).

Apart from Sofia University, there have been other Bulgarian institutions introducing Japanese language and culture in Bulgaria. One such institution is the Veliko Tarnovo University, which from 1993 offers a regular B.A. course in applied linguistics in Japanese, and since 1994, there has been a Centre for Japanese Language and Culture with a library section. Despite the fact that the course concentrates mostly on language studies, "students there organize cultural festivals to introduce Japanese culture to Bulgarians living in the north-east part of the country" and with each year "the effectiveness of such events seems to grow . . . and attract more and more attention" (Petkova, 2012, p. 7).

A highly essential institution promoting Japanese culture in Bulgaria has been the Bulgarian Academy of Sciences, where various specialists on Japan carry out research and publish their achievements. In addition, other independent scholars such as friends of the Japanese government, who have visited Japan to conduct research projects, also take part. They specialize in different areas, including architecture, international relations and politics, economics, medicine, and engineering. Most of them had been to Japan thanks to the variety of programs provided by the Japanese government, the Japan Foundation, the Ministry of Education, Culture, Sports, Science and Technology, JICA, the JSPS, and bilateral cooperation between universities and other institutions (Petkova, 2012, p. 7).

Another institution contributing greatly to the Japanese cultural promotion in Bulgaria has been the 18th "William Gladstone" High School in Sofia, which in 1992 became the first school in Europe to introduce Japanese language as compulsory subject in its secondary education program (Kandilarov, 2009, p. 347). Because of the increasing interest in the language, in 2005 the school also began to offer Japanese language courses from elementary education. In addition, the school established a Centre for Japanese Culture on its premises, where students are able to learn tea ceremony, *origami*, and games, as well as to attend Japanese culture classes. At the same time, as the number of students willing to enhance their knowledge about Japan continued to grow rapidly, many institutions in Bulgarian cities introduced programs for Japanese language and studies. This includes the "Vasil Levski" High School in Ruse, the 54th "St. Ivan Rilski" High School in Sofia, the 138th "Prof. Vasil Zlatarski" High School in Sofia, and others.

Significant public diplomacy actors have also been the Japanese language and studies students at universities and schools in Bulgaria. Each year the students organize events to promote Japanese culture. One such example is the annual Japanese Cultural Festival (*Nihon Bunka-sai*), which provides the general public with opportunities to observe Japanese traditions and arts, to taste Japanese cuisine, and to take part in workshops on calligraphy, games, and others. The growing number of visitors each year demonstrates the increasing interest in Japan of the Bulgarian people.

Besides the schools and universities in Bulgaria offering Japanese language and studies, in June 2003 a nongovernmental organization named "Association of Japanese Language Teachers in Bulgaria" was created. Its objective was not only to encourage the Japanese language education in Bulgaria, but also to contribute to the mutual understanding between the two countries (Kandilarov, 2009, p. 348).

An essential public diplomacy actor for promoting both Japanese language and culture in Bulgaria has been the St. Cyril and St. Methodius International Foundation. Since 1991, in partnership with the Japanese Ministry of Education, Culture, Sports, Science and Technology and the Japan Foundation, the St. Cyril and St. Methodius International Foundation has been conducting an active academic exchange, as well as a variety of programs (St. Cyril and St. Methodius International Foundation, n.d.). For instance, the Foundation cooperates with the Japanese Embassy in the selection of candidates for the Japanese government's *Monbukagakusho* Scholarship. Together with the Japanese Embassy and the Japan Foundation, it also organizes the Japanese Language Speech Contest and the Japanese-Language Proficiency Test (St. Cyril and St. Methodius International Foundation, n.d.).

Regarding the promotion of Japanese contemporary culture in Bulgaria, a major actor has been the National Club for Anime and Manga "NAKAMA", which was founded in 2008. Through the organization of various events, the club's aim has been to contribute to the popularization of Japanese animation and *manga* comic books in the country. For instance, as part of the "Days of Japanese Culture", in collaboration with the Japanese Embassy the club conducts a two-day annual festival called "Aniventure". The event gathers "fans of Japanese animation – anime, manga comics, console and computer games, martial arts, cosplay and provides a platform for young talents in the field of art, the production of costumes and accessories, theater, video editing and effects" (Aniventure, 2019). Although "Aniventure" is focused mainly on the presentation of Japanese modern culture, it conducts activities introducing traditional aspects as well. In addition to the "NAKAMA" club, sources of Japanese contemporary culture in Bulgaria have been the social media and TV programs broadcasting Japanese animation. There are also a few bookstores and shops from which *manga* and figurines can be purchased.

Japanese traditional culture has been widely promoted in Bulgaria through the Japan Foundation, as well as other Bulgarian and Japanese public diplomacy actors. These include the Japanese Embassy, the academic institutions emphasized earlier, and various clubs and associations. The Chado Urasenke Tankokai Bulgaria is a case in point. It was initially founded in 1992 as a club of people interested in tea ceremony and in 2001 was "officially registered with the Urasenke Head House as Bulgaria Association of Chado Urasenke Tankokai, Inc." (Chado Urasenke Tankokai Bulgaria, n.d.). Its aims are to disseminate the knowledge of *Chado*, the Way of Tea, and to contribute to the popularization of Japanese culture in Bulgaria through a variety of activities. For example, it holds demonstrations, public lectures, courses of tea ceremony, *ikebana* flower arrangement, Japanese cuisine, *origami* paper folding, calligraphy, *bonsai* tree, and *kitsuke* art of wearing kimono, translates and publishes books and articles on Japan, participates in TV programs, and so on. The association works both autonomously and in collaboration with various public diplomacy actors including the Embassy of Japan in Bulgaria, the St. Cyril and St. Methodius International Foundation, the 18th "William Gladstone" High School, and the Sofia University "St. Kliment Ohridski" (Chado Urasenke Tankokai Bulgaria, n.d.).

In addition to the Chado Urasenke Tankokai Bulgaria, other institutions have been also introducing Japanese traditional culture in Bulgaria. Such include the Soga Ikebana School, the Centre Ikuo Hirayama, and sports associations offering *go* and *shogi* games and diverse martial arts like *karate*, *sumo*, *aikido*, and *judo*.

Other public diplomacy actors contributing to the Japanese cultural promotion in Bulgaria include Bulgarian-Japanese friendship clubs and associations such as the Nihon-tomono-kai, the club of the Friends of Japan in Bulgaria, Veliko Turnovo's Japanese-Bulgarian Friendship Association, Varna's Japanese club "Kizuna", and others. Located in various cities in Bulgaria, these institutions provide opportunities to numerous people around the country to discover Japanese culture and to further develop their image on Japan.

The mass media has also been an essential public diplomacy actor for Japanese cultural promotion in Bulgaria. For instance, Bulgarian National Television (BNT) and Bulgarian National Radio (BNR) have been presenting a variety of programs on Japan such as the *Multicultural Dialogues* on BNR. These programs contribute to the mutual understanding between the two countries as well as provide Bulgarians with the opportunity to enhance their knowledge regarding Japanese scientific achievements, economic growth, nature, and sports (Petkova, 2012, p. 8).

The image of Japan and the future expectations from Japan in France and Bulgaria: exploring the insufficient points and less explored areas of Japanese soft power

As was observed earlier, Japan has been carrying out a full spectrum of public diplomacy initiatives in France and Bulgaria through the Japan Foundation and various public and private actors and institutions. However, what other cultural elements and aspects could be introduced for further strengthening Japanese soft power in the two countries?

To discover the insufficient points and the less explored areas of Japanese soft power in Europe, the author of this study conducted personal interviews with French and Bulgarian government officials and scholars as well as with other representatives of the young and middle-aged generations on the image of Japan and the future expectations from Japan in the two countries. Rather than interviewing numerous participants to generate numerical data and statistics typical for quantitative research, these interviews were of structured qualitative type aimed at collecting in-depth information on the topics from particular individuals and experts with considerable experience and familiarity with Japanese culture. The interviews were exploratory in nature with open-ended questions, allowing the respondents to provide unique answers and suggestions from their personal knowledge and perspective. In the case of France, the interviewees included a former ambassador of France to Japan, a scholar and former director of the Institut francais in Japan, a correspondent of *Le Monde* in Tokyo, an aeronautical engineer, a French language professor at the Sciences Po Rennes, a company manager, a digital consultant, an early childhood educator and kindergarten director, a professor of judo, a digital dentistry project manager, a musician, and an associate consultant in the pharmaceutical industry. In the case of Bulgaria, interviewees included a diplomat in charge of Bulgarian relations with Japan at the "Asia, Australia and Oceania" directorate of the Ministry of Foreign Affairs of Bulgaria, a lawyer/legal advisor at the Ministry of Foreign Affairs of Bulgaria, a senior diplomatic officer at the Ministry of Foreign Affairs of Bulgaria and political adviser in EU Common Security and Defense Policy (CSDP) missions, a former Bulgarian diplomat in Japan, a scholar, Japanese language teacher and author of various books on linguistics and cultural studies, a Japanese language high school teacher, a postdoctoral researcher in astrophysics, a professor of biotechnology at the University of Food Technologies in Plovdiv, a chief assistant professor at the Institute of Organic Chemistry with Centre of Phytochemistry (IOCCP), affiliated to the Bulgarian Academy of Sciences, a popular Bulgarian YouTuber, a web developer, a senior business analyst, and a landscape architect at the Japanese Embassy in Bulgaria.

The interviews consisted of 15 questions focused on the following topics – the image of Japan, the future expectations from Japan as well as the Japanese cultural aspects that are missing or necessary to be further introduced in France and Bulgaria, the main public diplomacy actors and sources from where the respondents have been learning about Japanese culture, and whether they have been more interested and familiar with traditional or contemporary Japanese culture.

Regarding the image of Japan in France, while more than half of the interviewees demonstrated to have a positive image of Japan, there have been a few negative perceptions as well. For instance, some respondents characterized Japan as a country with high seismicity, codified and reserved relationships, and difficult-to-understand relations between people. At the same time, various positive perceptions of Japan were pointed out. According to a scholar and former director of the Institut francais in Japan, Japan possesses a "stupendous nature, remarkable and very specific traditional culture, and strong personal ethics among individuals". Other respondents also described it as a country with beautiful landscapes that has preserved its traditions in parallel with its technological progress and that combines both tradition and modernism. The interviewees expressed various positive statements regarding Japanese society as well. For example, it was considered "hardworking, respectful, disciplined, and polite", which are "qualities that inspire confidence and facilitate relationships" (a French language professor at the Sciences Po Rennes). Similarly, an associate consultant in the pharmaceutical industry described Japanese people as "very sophisticated, respectful of the politeness in their social relationships and respectful of the hierarchy and the laws, industrious people with a substantial collective consciousness". All these positive perceptions of Japan have been formulated to a great extend due to the rich cultural promotion initiatives in France. Japanese public diplomacy has also contributed much to Japan's economic relations with France. As an associate consultant in the pharmaceutical industry highlights, Japanese public diplomacy "brings a very positive image of Japan with very good consequences for the Japanese business and industry, along with a great 'corporate image' of the Japanese companies and products".

In the case of Bulgaria, almost all of the interviewees revealed to have positive perceptions, except for a one slightly negative answer, characterizing Japan as a gender-unequal country. The remaining respondents pointed out various perceptions and aspects of Japanese culture and society, reflecting their positive overall image. For instance, a senior diplomatic officer at the Ministry of Foreign Affairs of Bulgaria considers Japan as a country with "rich history, unique culture, and traditional philosophy, which is worth studying and following". He also believes, "Japan managed to overcome the negatives of World War II and to excel as a constructive factor of peace and development internationally". According to a Bulgarian scholar, "Japan is a country with hardworking and honorable people, who possess a strong sense of duty, justice, and empathy". Another example of a positive image about Japan was demonstrated by a diplomat at the Ministry of Foreign Affairs of Bulgaria, considering it as a "highly developed country, which plays an important role in the shaping of the global agenda, has a leading economy, and is a great development assistance donor". Other interviewees emphasized Japanese language as an essential factor for the construction of their positive perception of Japan. One such example is a Japanese language high school teacher, who described it as a "lexically very rich language" and Japan as a country with beautiful nature "that combines centuries-old traditions with great technological advancement". There have been various positive statements regarding Japanese society as well. For instance, according to a chief assistant professor at the IOCCP, Japanese people are "very polite, well-behaved, hospitable". Similarly, a web developer considers Japanese society as "very disciplined, motivated, and organized". All these positive images of Japan demonstrate the efficiency of Japan's rich cultural promotion initiatives in Bulgaria. In addition, Japan's public diplomacy and the formulated perceptions on Japan have also contributed much to the Bulgarian-Japanese relations in various spheres. As a former Bulgarian diplomat in Japan highlights, Japanese public diplomacy has been

> a very important instrument in creating an atmosphere of mutual understanding and trust between Bulgarian and Japanese entrepreneurs, managers, and experts in various fields of economy to promote business and investment between the two countries, as well as to attract Bulgarian consumers to rely more on and prefer goods "made in Japan" compared to brands from other makers in Asia and worldwide.

Other essential points addressed in the interviews were the future expectations from Japan and the elements of Japanese culture that are missing or need to be further introduced in France and Bulgaria. In the case of France, it was revealed that although Japanese culture has been very well represented through various public diplomacy initiatives, there is still some space for improvement of Japan's soft power in the country. First, it was pointed out that there is a need for extending Japanese cultural activities outside Paris in order to increase Japan's cultural presence and reach out to a greater number of people. Second, it was emphasized that more Japanese art exhibitions as well as projects introducing Japanese architecture, innovation, and technologies should be conducted in France. Initiatives presenting Japanese diverse cuisine and martial arts were also demanded. Such projects are essential in order to nurture the popularity and interest in Japanese food in France and to maintain Japan's solid presence among other Asian countries like South Korea, which as a kindergarten director highlights, has been currently implementing a great number of activities to promote its cuisine in France. Third, there has also been a demand for initiatives introducing Japanese cultural values, including attitudes towards life and death, daily life and customs, relationships within families, gender relations and social relationships, as well as Japan's ecological choices and policies. Finally, it was emphasized that there should be more projects for increasing the number of Japanese people temporarily staying or living in France, since they have been greatly contributing to the promotion of Japanese culture in the country.

In the case of Bulgaria, it was revealed that there is still much space for improvement of Japan's soft power in the country. Various Japanese cultural elements were indicated to be missing or insufficiently introduced in Bulgaria. First, similar to the findings in the previous section, most of the interviewees, including a Bulgarian scholar, a diplomat, a lawyer/legal advisor at the Ministry of Foreign Affairs of Bulgaria, and a Japanese language high school teacher, pointed out the need for a Japanese cultural center in the country, which would regularly organize and host Japanese cultural activities. Second, there has been a demand for original Japanese language textbooks, dictionaries, and materials. In addition, a necessity for a greater variety of Japanese classic and contemporary books and magazines and broader access to reading and purchasing such literature in Bulgaria was also emphasized. As some interviewees revealed, although there has been a demand for Japanese *manga* comics, especially among the young generations, only a few shops in the country offer such books. Third, despite the growing interest in Japanese language and studies, the opportunities for studying Japanese language have been limited, particularly in educational institutions in cities outside the capital. As a chief assistant professor at the IOCCP highlights, to further strengthen its soft power in Bulgaria it is essential for Japan to "to encourage/get in contact with local universities and high schools outside the capital to include Japanese language in their programs". Fourth, the interviews revealed that Japanese achievements in the fields of technology, medicine, ecology, and science are also of great interest to Bulgarians but are still insufficiently represented. In order to further strengthen Japanese cultural presence in the country, it would be essential for Japan to focus on initiatives like lectures, conferences, seminars, and other projects addressing those aspects. Fifth, according to a former Bulgarian diplomat in Japan, another Japanese cultural element that needs to be further introduced in Bulgaria is Japan's classical theatre of *Noh, Kabuki,* and *Bunraku.* There has also been a necessity for a greater number of activities presenting Japanese traditional and contemporary culture such as Japanese art exhibitions and festivals. In addition to the existing clubs and associations around the country, more opportunities for learning Japanese visual and performance arts need to be provided as well. Another Japanese cultural element demanded to be introduced in Bulgaria is "Japanese cuisine, known worldwide as very balance, delicious and healthy, as well as some of its basic ingredients" (a former Bulgarian diplomat in Japan). While Japanese sushi has been gaining much popularity in the country, Bulgarian people still lack enough knowledge and experience of the diversity and healthy benefits of Japanese cuisine. Sixth, similar to the case of France, a necessity for expanding the Japanese cultural promotion initiatives in Bulgaria beyond the capital was also pointed out. For instance, the "Days of Japanese Culture" should "cover a wider area of cities and towns throughout the country so that more Bulgarian people could have access to the events" (a former Bulgarian diplomat in Japan). Another point emphasized during the interviews was the need for additional exchange programs for Bulgarian and Japanese high school and university students as well as for employees of Bulgarian companies and government officials. More "grants for scientific research and an easier access to scientific institutions in Japan" have also been sought (a chief assistant professor at the IOCCP). Those programs and initiatives have been crucial for the development of the positive image of Japan in Bulgaria and for the nurturing of the mutual understanding and bilateral relations between the two countries. At the same time, more projects for increasing the number of Japanese people temporarily staying or living in Bulgaria were recommended, since they have been greatly contributing to the promotion of Japanese culture in the country. Finally, the interviews revealed that various Japanese values such as daily life and customs, philosophies and attitudes towards life and death, attitudes towards nature, relationships within families, and social relationships have been insufficiently introduced in Bulgaria.

Other points discussed in the interviews included the main public diplomacy actors and the sources from where the respondents have been learning about Japanese culture in the two countries. In France, most of the interviewees indicated the Japan Foundation's Japan Cultural Institute in Paris. Other responses varied, pointing out the educational institutions in the country offering Japanese language and studies like INALCO, as well as bookstores, social media, and mass media, including television programs, periodicals, and newspapers like *Le Monde*. In the case of Bulgaria, the majority of the respondents identified bookstores around the country as essential public diplomacy actors, offering various books by Japanese classic and contemporary authors. This tendency is to a great extent due to the Japan Foundation's financial assistance for the translation and publication of such works. The interviewees also pointed out the scientific bodies and the educational institutions offering Japanese language and studies, as well as the Japanese Embassy, the Japan Foundation, mass media, social media, and associations and clubs such as the Nihon-tomono-kai, the Club of the Friends of Japan in Bulgaria, as other significant Japanese cultural promotion actors.

Finally, the two countries' interviewees were asked to reveal whether they have been more interested in and familiar with traditional or contemporary Japanese culture. In France, most of the respondents favored the elements from traditional culture, fewer were interested in both types, and just a few preferred contemporary trends. In the case of Bulgaria, the majority of the interviewees possessed a greater interest and familiarity with aspects of Japanese traditional culture, while considerably fewer preferred contemporary culture, and a few were equally attracted to both types. Taking into account the fact that the interviewees were representatives from various generations ranging from the European elite to the young and the middle-aged generations, it could be assumed that to some extent the interest in and familiarity with Japanese traditional culture in both countries tend to be a little higher than that of the modern trends. However, as this result was formulated based on qualitative interviews rather than on quantitative statistical data, further investigation might be necessary to draw a more profound conclusion on this topic.

An outlook for the future

As was demonstrated in the previous discussions, apart from the Japan Foundation there have been various cultural promotion actors in France and Bulgaria that have been contributing to the increase of Japanese cultural presence in the two countries. It was revealed that some of those actors, such as the Ministry of Foreign Affairs, the Japanese Embassy, local educational and scientific bodies, and other public and private institutions, have been collaborating with the Foundation on the implementation of Japanese cultural activities in various spheres. On the other hand, there have also been many other actors promoting Japanese culture, with potential for cooperation with the Foundation, which have been acting autonomously or which have been carrying out joint projects on rare occasions, as was the case of Japonismes 2018. Some of those actors, like the Wakaba Association, have been conducting similar or overlapping activities with those of the Japan Foundation. In addition, there has been a lack of a common strategy among the separate public diplomacy actors as well as a major institution facilitating an integrated network for regular collaboration between those actors. At the same time, as the discussions with the interviewees demonstrated, despite the rich palette of cultural promotion initiatives by both the Japan Foundation and other public diplomacy actors, there still have been some missing or insufficient points of Japan's soft power in France and Bulgaria. In order to compensate for those areas and increase Japan's cultural presence in the regions, it would be vital for Japan to design new cultural promotion projects, whose implementation would require new policies for enhanced collaboration networks among the Japanese cultural promotion actors in both countries. Therefore, to strengthen the efficiency of Japan's public diplomacy in Europe, Japan should establish a Public-Private Partnership Platform for cooperation facilitated by a central public diplomacy actor that will unify and coordinate the collaborations among the involved public and private actors and their activities. Such actors would include members from related ministries and agencies, various public and private institutions, and nongovernmental organizations. Taking into account the contributions and the role of the Japan Foundation emphasized in previous sections, this study proposes the Foundation as major public diplomacy actor facilitating such a Public-Private Partnership Platform. Together with the Foundation's close cooperation with the Ministry of Foreign Affairs and other actors revealed in this study, the Platform's partnerships network should expand to include crucial Japanese institutions like the Cabinet Office, the Ministry of Economy, Trade and Industry, the Agency for Cultural Affairs, and the Japan National Tourism Organization. Other members should be also various public and private institutions and nongovernmental organizations related to Japanese cultural promotion. At the same time, the participants involved in the Platform should facilitate additional partnerships and collaboration channels with Japanese and local public and private actors introducing Japanese culture in France and Bulgaria. The Japan Foundation's Japan Cultural Institute could be utilized as a center and a venue for both the conduct of the Foundations' initiatives and for the planning and coordination of the Public-Private Partnership Platform's integrated cultural promotion projects. In the case of Bulgaria, where a Cultural Institute does not exist yet, the establishment of such an institution or an office of the Foundation would be also essential. Figure 5.1 demonstrates the suggested Public-Private Partnership Platform:

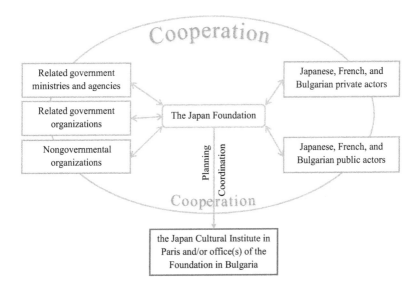

Figure 5.1 A Desired Form of Public-Private Partnership Platform for an Integrated Japanese Public Diplomacy in France and Bulgaria

As part of its Cool Japan Strategy, the Cabinet Office has launched a Cool Japan Public-Private Partnership Platform with the aim of strengthening the "collaborations between the public and private sectors and among different industries in the Cool Japan fields and effectively promote Cool Japan initiatives as a nation" (Cool Japan Strategy Promotion Council, 2015, p. 9). The actors involved in the Platform include government bodies and private sector companies and organizations from various private-sector fields, including the content industry, dining and food products, tourism, manufacturing, and distribution (Cabinet Office, 2015). This Public-Private Partnership Platform's purpose has been to serve as "a venue for forming and matching dynamic collaborative Cool Japan projects" and "a venue for sharing cutting-edge practices (such as knowledge on merchandising content)" (Cool Japan Strategy Promotion Council, 2015, p. 9). It enables the Cabinet Office to more efficiently promote Japanese culture and fulfill its Cool Japan Strategy's goals through close collaborations with various public and private actors. Therefore, the participation of the Cabinet Office and its current partners in the suggested Public-Private Partnership Platform facilitated by the Japan Foundation would be beneficial for the strengthening of both Japan's cultural presence and its economic relations with Europe. The broad network of actors would collaborate on the conduct of a more purposeful Japanese public diplomacy in Europe, as well as on the increase of the variety and the number of Japanese cultural initiatives, introducing cultural aspects in diverse fields. At the same time, the growing interest and attraction abroad in Japanese cultural elements and products would contribute greatly to Japanese economic growth and soft power in the region.

Together with the integration of the organizations and projects, the establishment of the Public-Private Partnership Platform would bring various benefits for the development of the Japanese public diplomacy as well. First, the involved actors could regularly share their experiences in terms of Japanese cultural promotion and reveal both the effective and the insufficient points of the implemented initiatives. This regular exchange of practices and results would suggest innovative strategies for further improvement of the projects as well as for the introduction of Japanese cultural aspects to a broader extent. At the same time, these unified efforts would contribute to the recognition and the creation of new and more advanced future Japanese public diplomacy directions. Second, the Public-Private Partnership Platform would provide opportunities for the Japanese public diplomacy actors that have been carrying out similar or overlapping initiatives to work together on the clear separation of their activities as well as on the coordination of the projects' content. As mentioned earlier, such has been the case of the Japan Foundation and the Agency for Cultural Affairs. It would be essential for both institutions to collaborate on the resolution of these issues in order to enhance their efficiency and economize funds spent on similar projects. In addition to these points, the establishment of the Public-Private Partnership Platform would bring various profits to the Japanese cultural sector as a whole. As the European Union (n.d.) highlights,

> in the cultural domain partnerships involving the government, the business sector and a wide variety of institutions from civil society have enormous potential in finding innovative solutions for the delivery of social and cultural services, the development of human resources, and the promotion and protection of cultural heritage.

Instituting Public-Private Partnership Platform partnerships for collaboration between the Japan Foundation and the involved actors would enable Japan to design new integrated public diplomacy initiatives in response to aforementioned missing or insufficient points of Japan's soft power in France and Bulgaria. The participants could also establish additional networks and channels for cooperation with local institutions and actors from the public and private sectors, thus extending the scopes of Japanese cultural promotion in the two countries and reaching out to a greater number of people. Considering the expectations from Japan and the areas indicated as necessary to be further introduced according to the interviewees, this study suggests the following project proposals for implementation either autonomously by the Japan Foundation or through collaborations between actors involved in the Public-Private Partnership Platform.

Prospective future projects in France

(1) In response to the necessity of increasing the Japanese cultural presence outside Paris, as was emphasized in earlier sections, it is essential for the Japan Foundation to establish additional branches or offices of its Cultural Institute in various French cities, where it could carry out and host cultural initiatives on a regular basis. For instance, there could be exhibitions, conferences, and workshops, as well as Japanese language- and culture-related courses, including tea ceremony, calligraphy, *ikebana* flower arrangement, *origami* paper folding, and many others, providing a greater number of people with the opportunity to increase their knowledge of Japan. At the same time, together with the Japan Cultural Institute in Paris, these branches could coordinate the integrated activities of the Japan Foundation's Public-Private Partnership Platform within a wider area of France. This would also enable the members of the Platform to establish new partnerships with various local public and private institutions and actors.

(2) Another point emphasized was the interest in projects introducing Japanese architecture, innovation, and technologies in France. To compensate for these demands and further strengthen Japan's cultural presence in the country, the following project proposals could be suggested. First, through the Public-Private Partnership Platform, the Japan Foundation could maintain regular cooperation with Japanese and French educational institutions and scientific bodies to conduct joint projects such as lectures, conferences, and symposiums discussing Japanese architecture, innovation, and technologies. Initiatives introducing these aspects such as exhibitions, demonstrations, and lectures could be held at the Japan Cultural Institute in Paris as well. The Institute could provide particular literature on these topics at its library, too. In addition, to further present these elements, the Foundation could work with other potential public and private partner institutions in France to implement joint cultural activities and events. One such partner could be the Japan Science and Technology Agency, which has been offering information on science and technology and carrying out initiatives to strengthen the Japanese presence in France and other European countries.

At the same time, the establishment of more exchange programs between Japanese and French educational institutions specialized in the spheres of architecture, innovation, and technologies would be essential as well. The programs would not only develop specialists on Japan in France, but also contribute to the expansion of the French and Japanese research networks.

Another project proposal is to establish branch campuses of Japanese universities in France, specialized particularly in the spheres of architecture, innovation, and technologies. As was demonstrated earlier, there have been various French institutions offering Japanese language and studies but no branch campuses of Japanese universities yet.

For the planning and the organization of this initiative, Japan could facilitate collaboration networks between Japanese and French public and private actors through the previously emphasized Public-Private Partnership Platform. These would include the governments of Japan and France, Japanese specialized educational institutions such as the Tokyo Institute of Technology, the University of Tokyo, the Osaka University, the Kyoto University, the Waseda University, and other related actors.

This initiative would enable students from both France and other European countries to not only acquire an academic degree, but also further develop their perceptions of Japan. At the established Japanese university branch campuses, there could be programs in English, Japanese, or French languages in the curricula, providing opportunities for students from various countries to enroll and study in a diverse multicultural environment. In addition, together with the main academic programs, in cooperation with the Japan Foundation, the branch campuses could offer Japanese language- and culture-related courses. Japanese scholars and experts could also be invited by the Foundation to carry out lectures and conferences on various topics introducing Japanese achievements in the fields of technology, innovation, and architecture. At the same time, exchange and study abroad programs at those universities' main campuses in Japan could be also available, enabling the students to experience Japanese culture and develop relationships.

The implementation of this project would bring a variety of benefits to Japan. First, together with the financial profits, it would contribute to an increasingly positive image of Japan and the prestige of its educational institutions in Europe. This could also lead to a growing number of European students interested in studying at universities in Japan. In addition, the creative personnel graduating from the universities' branch campuses would work for the future promotion and advancement of innovation and technologies as well as for the introduction of Japanese achievements in those fields in Europe. Some might also continue pursuing further education or a career in Japan, thus contributing to the country's research network expansion and industrial development.

(3) To further strengthen Japan's culinary presence in France, various cuisine-centered projects could be implemented, especially with a focus on the diversity and healthy benefits of Japanese cuisine. First, more films featuring these aspects could be broadcasted together with the publication of cuisine articles in online magazines and social media in France. Second, cooking classes, lectures, demonstrations, workshops, food markets, and food festivals could be held in France by related Japanese actors, including the Japan Foundation, the Cabinet Office, the Ministry of Economy, Trade and Industry, and JETRO both autonomously and in collaboration with local actors like the France-Japan friendship associations. In addition, a greater number of internship programs for French culinary school graduates and industry professionals could be offered at Japanese restaurants in Japan, such as the aforementioned "Human Resource Development for Japanese Cuisine/Food Culture" project. Third, to develop human resources for Japanese cuisine, branch campuses of Japanese culinary schools could be also created in France. This initiative would be again organized with the close collaboration of Japanese and French actors through the Public-Private Partnership Platform, including the governments of Japan and France and Japanese specialized culinary institutions such as the Japan Culinary Institute, the Tokyo Sushi Academy, the TSUJI Culinary Institute, and others. These campuses would also function as hubs for disseminating information in France. Finally, to further promote culinary studies in Japan, the conduct of a greater number of expositions and orientations in France introducing the available courses at such culinary institutes and academies would be crucial.

(4) As mentioned earlier, Japan should focus on the further promotion of Japanese values in France. Since the discussions revealed some negative perceptions of Japan and misunderstandings among the French public, particularly in terms of its social relationships, the conduct of such projects would be also essential for transforming these perceptions and strengthening the mutual understanding between the two countries. These initiatives would be beneficial for maintaining interest in Japan in a long-term perspective as well.

To compensate for the demand of introducing Japanese cultural values in France, various activities could be suggested for implementation both autonomously by the Japan Foundation as well as in collaboration with Japanese and French actors through the Public-Private Partnership Platform's network. First, the Foundation and the Japanese Embassy could provide films and literature featuring Japanese attitudes towards life and death, daily life, customs, and social relationships. These materials could be presented both at the Foundation's Cultural Institute in Paris and in cooperation with Japanese and French actors such as the media. Second, Japanese values could be promoted through lectures and workshops held at the Institute, at French primary schools, colleges, high schools, and universities offering Japanese language and studies as well as during cultural festivals and events like the Japan Expo. The lectures could demonstrate various cultural aspects, including social relationships, Japanese healthy lifestyle, disaster management systems, and environmental policies and technologies. The workshops held at French educational institutions could be focused, for example, on the introduction of specific Japanese school manners, systems, and customs, such as the healthy meals and nutrition education, the emphasis on teaching morals and ethics, the students' responsibility for cleaning the schools by themselves, and their common efforts and preparations for the conduct of festivals. These initiatives would be beneficial for strengthening the positive image of Japan and its cultural presence in France. Third, the Japan Foundation could implement joint projects with the Cabinet Office, which has also been working to introduce Japanese values abroad. The Intellectual Property Headquarters of the Cabinet Office has begun a "Nihon Gatari-Sho" project entrusted to the "Editorial Engineering Laboratory", with the aim of presenting a model for discussing "Cool Japan" from the perspective of "Japan Concepts" and that "can be referred to when compiling stories and contexts that will benefit the attractive conveyance and deployment of products, services, tourist areas, local cultures and so on" (Cabinet Office, 2018). Both autonomously and in collaboration with the Cabinet Office, the Foundation could carry out expositions, events, and lectures at the Japan Cultural Institute in Paris, demonstrating such historical and cultural backgrounds of Japanese values, arts, and products. It could also contribute to the further dissemination of the "Nihon Gatari-Sho" narrative modules in Europe. In addition, the Japan Foundation could introduce new courses and learning programs at the Institute as well as invite specialists to present various contexts of Japanese culture. Together with its local partners, the Foundation could also regularly conduct surveys on the French perceptions of particular Japanese values and the further demands and expectations from Japan in France. The feedback from these studies and the exchanges between the Cabinet Office, the Japan Foundation, and other involved actors would contribute to the advancement of the implemented projects as well as to the development of new initiatives.

(5) In response to the demand for further increasing the number of Japanese people temporarily staying or living in France, the following initiatives could be suggested. First, the bilateral collaboration on the provision of more career opportunities for Japanese people in France and the establishment of a system regularly presenting available job positions as well as the career requirements of both the French companies and Japanese people would be essential. Japan could cooperate with local institutions in France on the conduct of surveys with Japanese nationals working in the country on the factors, conditions, and prerequisites for pursuing their current careers, as well as on their future expectations and demands. Japanese people interested in working in France could be interviewed as well. At the same time, questionnaires could be distributed to French companies and institutions, currently cooperating or with potential for further exchanges with Japan, on the career opportunities offered for Japanese people. For the conduct of such studies, the Public-Private Partnership Platform would be crucial. Through the established networks, the Japan Foundation and the Japanese Embassy could cooperate with local institutions in France and Japan to carry out surveys, while utilizing the Japan Cultural Institute in Paris as a hub for processing, publishing, and regularly updating the accumulated data. The statistics would be beneficial in providing broader access to career opportunities in France, as well as in further increasing Japan's presence through the attraction of Japanese human resources. Second, Japan could work on the additional expansion of the study abroad and exchange programs with French educational institutions. In order to develop new opportunities, surveys with students and scholars from both countries could be conducted on the spheres of their academic interests and the currently available study abroad programs in relation to these fields. Similarly, the Japan Foundation's partners involved in the Public-Private Partnership Platform as well as the Cultural Institute in Paris could be utilized for the planning and implementation of the research. Feedback from the studies would reveal the less explored areas and the two countries' mutual expectations, suggesting

new perspectives for inter-university, school, and other related institutional agreements for study abroad and exchange programs.

Prospective future projects in Bulgaria

(1) As emphasized in the previous section, to provide systematic and regular Japanese cultural promotion throughout the year, the Japan Foundation's Japan Cultural Institute or a similar Japanese cultural center should be established in Bulgaria. Together with a broad spectrum of cultural activities in the fields of visual and performing arts and courses on Japanese language and culture that could be implemented or hosted at the Institute, it could be utilized as a coordinator of the Foundation's Public-Private Partnership Platform's integrated activities in Bulgaria. It could also focus on the presentation of demanded Japanese traditional and contemporary cultural elements in Bulgaria already highlighted, such as Japan's classical theatre of *Noh*, *Kabuki*, and *Bunraku*. In addition, to expand Japan's cultural presence outside the capital, further partnerships with local public and private institutions could be initiated through the Institute and the Platform. These collaborations would provide broader opportunities for Japanese cultural activities in Bulgaria.

(2) To compensate for the necessity of original Japanese literature and Japanese language textbooks and materials in Bulgaria, the following activities could be suggested. First, books and magazines could be provided regularly through the Japanese Embassy and the Japan Foundation and disseminated in cooperation with public and private partners around the country such as local educational institutions and libraries. At the same time, there could be more private initiatives for opening specialized stores for Japanese classic and contemporary books, Japanese language textbooks and dictionaries, and *manga* comic books. Events dedicated to literature promotion, like book markets and festivals, could also be organized by the Foundation and related institutions including the National Club for Anime and Manga "NAKAMA". Such practices could be included at the annual schedule of the "Days of Japanese Culture" as well.

(3) In response to the insufficient Japanese language and studies courses outside the capital city of Sofia, the following initiatives could be suggested. First, through the network of the Public-Private Partnership Platform, the Japan Foundation and the Japanese Embassy could carry out research in various cities on the perspectives, conditions, and students' interests and demands for studying Japanese language at local universities and schools. Based on the findings, Japan could work in cooperation with municipalities and educational institutions on the introduction of such courses. At the same time, it would be essential to conduct initiatives encouraging Bulgarian

graduates in Japanese language and studies to teach at the newly established departments in the country. For example, an online platform presenting the available career opportunities at local public and private institutions seeking such specialists could be created. Together with the Japan Foundation, the Japanese government could also work on the expansion of the number of Japanese language and studies specialists and teaching personnel dispatched in Bulgaria. At the same time, the development of more private initiatives and institutions offering Japanese language around the country could be also encouraged.

(4) Another point emphasized previously was the interest in projects introducing Japanese achievements in the fields of medicine, technologies, ecology, and science in Bulgaria. In response to these demands, the following initiatives could be suggested. First, through the Public-Private Partnership Platform, the Japan Foundation could maintain regular cooperation with Japanese and Bulgarian educational institutions and scientific bodies on conducting joint projects such as lectures, conferences, and symposiums focused on these topics. Second, similar to the case of France, Japan should work on the provision of more exchange programs between Japanese and Bulgarian institutions in the spheres of medicine, technologies, and ecology as well as on the establishment of branch campuses of specialized Japanese universities in Bulgaria. Significant for the planning and organization of these initiatives would again be the bilateral collaboration and networks forming from the Public-Private Partnership Platform.

(5) Concerning the demand for further increasing the number of Japanese people temporarily staying or living in Bulgaria, the following initiatives could be suggested. Similar to that of France, Bulgarian-Japanese collaboration on the provision of more career opportunities for Japanese people in Bulgaria and the establishment of a system regularly presenting available job positions as well as the requirements of both Bulgarian companies and Japanese people would be essential. Japan could cooperate with local institutions in Bulgaria to conduct surveys with Japanese nationals working in the country on their current careers and future expectations. Japanese people interested in working in Bulgaria could be interviewed as well. At the same time, questionnaires could be distributed to Bulgarian companies and institutions that are currently cooperating or with potential for further interactions with Japan. For the planning and conduct of these studies, the bilateral collaboration through the Public-Private Partnership Platform's network would be crucial. Second, as was highlighted earlier, it is essential for Japan to work on the expansion of the study abroad and exchange programs with Bulgarian educational institutions. In order to develop new inter-university and school opportunities and discover the two countries' mutual expectations, surveys with students and scholars from Bulgaria and

Japan could be conducted on the spheres of their academic interests and the currently available study abroad programs in relation to these fields. Similarly, collaborations forming from the Public-Private Partnership Platform would be beneficial for the implementation of such research.

The establishment of an office of the Japan Society for the Promotion of Science, conducting a variety of related projects, would be crucial for the strengthening the Bulgarian-Japanese academic and scientific exchange as well as for the increase of the number of Japanese people in Bulgaria. Initiatives like university visits, conferences, and forums organized by the JSPS Strasbourg Office in France are a case in point. In addition, bilateral cooperation on the development of a regular budget airline between Bulgaria and Japan would also be highly contributory to the increase of Bulgarian-Japanese exchanges and tourism.

(6) Another point emphasized earlier was the Bulgarian people's insufficient knowledge and experience in terms of Japanese cuisine. Similar to the case of France, to further strengthen Japan's culinary presence in Bulgaria, various cuisine-centered projects could be implemented through the Public-Private Partnership Platform's network. Such include the broadcasting of specialized programs in cooperation with Bulgarian media, publications of cuisine articles in online magazines and social media, and the promotion of Japanese cooking recipe books, as well as the conduct of cooking classes, lectures, demonstrations, workshops, food markets, and food festivals. These initiatives could be organized by related Japanese institutions like the Japanese Embassy and the Japan Foundation, both autonomously and in collaboration with local actors like the Nihon-tomono-kai, the Club of the Friends of Japan in Bulgaria. Other activities could also include the provision of internship programs for Bulgarian culinary school graduates and industry professionals at Japanese restaurants in Japan and academic exchange programs, as well as the establishment of branch campuses of Japanese culinary schools in Bulgaria. Organized through close bilateral cooperation via the Public-Private Partnership Platform, these initiatives would develop essential human resources disseminating broad aspects of Japanese culinary culture in Bulgaria.

(7) As demonstrated previously, there has been much interest in Japanese values in Bulgaria, but not enough activities representing these aspects. In response to this demand, various initiatives could be suggested for implementation both autonomously by the Japan Foundation as well as in collaboration with Japanese and Bulgarian actors through the Public-Private Partnership Platform's network. Similar to the case of France, the Foundation and the Japanese Embassy could provide films and literature featuring Japanese attitudes towards life and death, daily life, customs, and social relationships. Japanese values could also be presented through lectures and

workshops held at Bulgarian educational institutions and during the "Days of Japanese Culture". For instance, the lectures could introduce Japanese healthy lifestyle, attitudes towards nature, environmental policies, and disaster management systems. Features like *omotenashi* Japanese hospitality and *wabi-sabi* aesthetics of imperfection could also be represented. Similar to the case of France, workshops conducted at Bulgarian schools and universities could focus on specific aspects of Japan such as school manners, systems, customs, and student's healthy meals and nutrition education. At the same time, Japanese values could be promoted through the dissemination of the Cabinet Office's "Nihon Gatari-Sho" narrative modules with the support of the Japanese Embassy. The encouragement of publications and studies on such topics by Bulgarian scholars would be essential as well. Much beneficial would be the Japan Foundation's assistance for translation and publication of books on Japan in Bulgaria.

Taking into account the suggested initiatives, it could be assumed that for the systematic organization and implementation of future Japanese cultural projects in France and Bulgaria, the establishment of such a Public-Private Partnership Platform is vital. The coordination and collaboration between the actors from the public and private sectors developing from this integrated approach would contribute to the efficiency of Japanese public diplomacy and to the expansion of Japan's presence in the countries. In addition, these public-private partnerships could serve as a framework of further systemic initiatives for the Japan Foundation both autonomously and in cooperation with Japanese and local actors in Europe and worldwide.

References

Aniventure. (2019). *About Aniventure*. Retrieved February 24, 2019, from https://aniventure.net/en/info/about-aniventure

Cabinet Office. (2015). The Cool Japan Public-Private Partnership Platform. *Cool Japan Strategy*. Retrieved May 9, 2020, from www.cao.go.jp/cool_japan/english/platform_en/platform_en.html

Cabinet Office. (2018). Nihon-Gatari-Sho. *Cool Japan Strategy*. Retrieved June 6, 2020, from www.cao.go.jp/cool_japan/english/report_en/report_en.html

Chado Urasenke Tankokai, Bulgaria. (n.d.). *Chado Urasenke Tankokai Bulgaria*. Retrieved February 24, 2019, from www.urasenke-bulgaria.net/?inc=page&id=189&s_id=1&lang=en

Cool Japan Strategy Promotion Council. (2015, June 17). *Cool Japan strategy public-private collaboration initiative*. Retrieved from www.cao.go.jp/cool_japan/english/pdf/published_document2.pdf

European Union. (n.d.). *Influence of culture on social development through public and private partnership*. Culture & Creativity EU-Eastern Partnership Programme. Retrieved September 29, 2020, from www.culturepartnership.eu/upload/

editor/2017/Factsheets/Pdf-12/12_Influence%20of%20culture%20on%20 social%20development.%20Public%20and%20private%20partnership_ENG.pdf

Fondation Franco-Japonaise Sasakawa. (n.d.). *Présentation de la Fondation* [Presentation of the foundation]. Retrieved February 13, 2019, from http://ffjs.org/ decouvrir/?lang=fr

Japan Expo. (2018). *France – Japan: A longstanding affinity.* SEFA Event. Retrieved January 29, 2019, from www.japan-expo-paris.com/en/menu_info/ introduction_100984.htm

Japan Science and Technology Agency France, PARIS Office. (n.d.). *About us.* Retrieved February 12, 2019, from www.jst.go.jp/inter/paris/JST_About_UK.html

Japan Society for the Promotion of Science. (n.d.). *About us.* Retrieved February 12, 2019, from www.jsps.go.jp/english/aboutus/index2.html

JSPS Strasbourg office. (n.d.). *Activités* [Activities]. Retrieved February 12, 2019, from http://jsps.unistra.fr/activites/

Kandilarov, E. (2009). *Bulgariya i Yaponiya. Ot Studenata voina kum XXI vek* [Bulgaria and Japan: From the cold war towards the 21st century]. Sofia: D. Yakov.

Kaneko, M., & Kitano, M. (2014). *Paburikku Dipuromashī Senryaku: Imēji wo Kisou Kokka-kan Gēmu ni Ikani Shōrisuruka* [Public diplomacy strategy: How to win an interstate game competing for images]. PHP Kenkyuusho.

Kinki Bureau of Economy, Trade and Industry. (2018). *Challenge local Cool Japan in Pari* [Challenge local Cool Japan in Paris]. Retrieved February 21, 2019, from www.kansai.meti.go.jp/3-2sashitsu/CCkansai/france/challenge2/sentei.html

Kitera, M. (2018). Présentation de l'Ambassadeur [Presentation of the ambassador]. *Ambassade du Japon en France* [Embassy of Japan in France]. Retrieved February 13, 2019, from www.fr.emb-japan.go.jp/itpr_fr/presentation-ambassadeur.html

Le Cordon Bleu. (n.d.). *Japanese cuisine bursary programme.* Retrieved February 20, 2019, from www.cordonbleu.edu/news/japanese-cuisine-bursary-programme/en

Manga Café. (2018). *A propos* [About]. Retrieved February 18, 2019, from www. mangacafe.fr/a-propos/

Ministry of Economy, Trade and Industry. (n.d.). *Japanese food culture promotion project in France.* Retrieved February 19, 2019, from www.meti.go.jp/english/ policy/mono_info_service/creative_industries/pdf/130201_01n.pdf

Ministry of Foreign Affairs of Japan. (2014a). *Japan international MANGA award.* Retrieved February, 18, 2019, from www.manga-award.mofa.go.jp/index_e.html

Ministry of Foreign Affairs of Japan. (2014b). *About the MANGA award.* Japan International MANGA Award. Retrieved February, 18, 2019, from www. manga-award.mofa.go.jp/contents/whats_e.html

Ministry of Foreign Affairs of Japan. (2019, February 27). *Press conference by foreign press secretary Takeshi Osuga.* Retrieved from www.mofa.go.jp/press/ kaiken/kaiken4e_000612.html

Ministry of Foreign Affairs of Japan. (2020, August 27). *Japan-France Relations (Basic Data).* Japan-France Relations. Retrieved January 31, 2019, from https:// www.mofa.go.jp/region/europe/france/data.html

National Diet Library, Japan. (n.d.). *Section 1: Cuisine. Modern Japan and France – adoration, encounter and interaction.* Retrieved February 19, 2019, from www. ndl.go.jp/france/en/column/s2_1.html

Petkova, G. (2012). Promotion and Reception of Japanese Culture in Bulgaria. *Seijo CJS Reports*, no. 1. Tokyo: Center for Glocal Studies, Seijo University.

St. Cyril and St. Methodius International Foundation. (n.d.). *Major programs and activities.* Retrieved February 24, 2019, from www.cmfnd.org/?page_id=1529

Wakaba Association. (2019). *Matsuri.* Retrieved February 13, 2019, from www. association-wakaba.com/?-Matsuri-

Watanabe, H. (2018). The 160th Anniversary of Franco-Japanese Diplomatic Relations: How France Discovered Japonisme. Discuss Japan, Japan Foreign Policy Forum, Ministry of Foreign Affairs of Japan, *Diplomacy*, 49. https://www. japanpolicyforum.jp/pdf/2018/no49/DJweb_49_dip_03.pdf

ZOOM Japon. (n.d.). *A propos* [About]. Retrieved February 1, 2019, from http:// zoomjapon.info/apropos/

6 Conclusion

This book examined Japan's soft power and public diplomacy, with an emphasis on its characteristics, current issues, and future prospects.

From the perspective of its strategy, desired image, and cultural aspects promoted abroad, Japanese public diplomacy was described as "warm power" or "kind power". These terms illustrated Japan's policy since World War II, presenting it as a harmonious and friendly country that combines tradition with modern culture. From the viewpoint of its organization and structure, Japanese public diplomacy was also named "scattered power". This concept reflected its current state, characterized by the lack of integration and coordination among the separate public and private actors and their initiatives. Rethinking and transforming this state into a "unified power" policy has been crucial for enhancing the efficiency of Japanese public diplomacy and cultural presence abroad.

In response to this issue, the study analyzed an integrated approach for Japanese public diplomacy through public-private partnerships facilitated by the Japan Foundation.

With a focus on the Japan Foundation's activities between 1973 and 2018 in France and Bulgaria, the study explored its contributions as well as certain public and private partners for Japanese cultural promotion in the two countries. In Bulgaria, these included the Embassy of Japan in Sofia, the St. Cyril and St. Methodius International Foundation, the Sofia University "St. Kliment Ohridski", and friendship associations like the Fukuyama Bulgaria Association. In France, the Foundation has been cooperating with the Ministry of Foreign Affairs of Japan, the Embassy of Japan in Paris, JETRO, the Japan National Tourism Organization, the French agency Campus France, the French film organization Cinematheque Francaise, various educational institutions like Paris Diderot University, the College de France, the Lille 2 University of Health and Law, the National Institute of Oriental Languages and Civilizations, and others. It was emphasized that essential for the successful organization and implementation of the Japan

DOI: 10.4324/9781003006251-6

Foundation's projects throughout the years were its systematic efforts and collaboration with these public and private actors. The study also discussed the strong and the insufficient points of the Foundation's cultural promotion in the two countries. It was discovered that the Foundation has been considerably more active and diverse in its activities in France, due to the contribution of the Japan Cultural Institute in Paris. Based on the findings, the study provided a framework of suggestions concerning the future projects of the Japan Foundation in France and Bulgaria for further increasing Japan's cultural presence.

Other points examined in the study were the Japan Foundation's role, advantages, and factors, evidencing its high potential for becoming Japan's leading public diplomacy actor in Europe. First, one such factor was the broad network of public and private partners for cultural promotion in Europe and worldwide, with whom the Foundation has been cooperating to realize various initiatives. Second, the Foundation's special role during the Japonismes 2018 event as a secretariat in charge of the planning and implementation of the project was also emphasized. Other factors revealing its potential included the purpose of its establishment in 1972, as well as the designated functions of the Foundation during Japan's Central Government Reform in 2001. The study also demonstrated specific advantages of the Japan Foundation in comparison with other public diplomacy actors and its role for nurturing interest towards Japan in Europe in a long-term perspective.

Taking into account the aforementioned points and its activities and contributions in France and Bulgaria, the study suggested the Japan Foundation as a major public diplomacy actor facilitating a Public-Private Partnership Platform in Europe. The Platform was considered crucial for the increase of Japanese soft power on the continent. In line with this, the study explored other public and private actors promoting Japanese culture in Europe with potential for future cooperation with the Japan Foundation as members of the Platform. These included related government ministries, agencies and organizations, and nongovernmental organizations, as well as various public and private institutions such as the Cabinet Office, the Ministry of Economy, Trade and Industry of Japan, the Agency for Cultural Affairs, and the Japan National Tourism Organization. At the same time, the study highlighted the importance for the participants involved in the Platform to facilitate additional partnerships and collaboration channels with Japanese and local public and private institutions introducing Japanese culture in France and Bulgaria. These included the Japan Society for the Promotion of Science, the Japan Science and Technology Agency, Bulgarian and French educational institutions offering Japanese language and studies, the Japan Student Services Organization, the Bulgarian Academy of Sciences, various clubs promoting Japanese arts, Bulgarian-Japanese and French-Japanese friendship associations, other associations, clubs, and foundations like the Wakaba Association, the Fondation Franco-Japonaise Sasakawa, and the Nihon-tomono-kai, the mass media, bookstores offering Japanese classic and contemporary literature and *manga* comic books, online journals with articles on Japan, and others. Some of these institutions have been acting autonomously, while others have been conducting joint projects with the Japan Foundation on rare occasions, as was the case of Japonismes 2018. The future systematic cooperation between the Japan Foundation and these actors through the Public-Private Partnership is significant for the strengthening of the efficiency of Japanese public diplomacy in Europe. The study also suggested the Japan Foundation's Japan Cultural Institute and its offices to be utilized as hubs and venues for both the conduct of the Foundations' initiatives and for the planning and coordination of the Public-Private Partnership Platform's integrated projects. In addition, various benefits of this Public-Private Partnership Platform were pointed out as well. These included opportunities for regular exchange of practices and results between the involved actors, revealing both the effective and the insufficient points of the implemented initiatives. These collaborations would also contribute to the creation of innovative strategies for further improvement of the projects and for the introduction of Japanese cultural aspects to a broader extent. At the same time, these unified efforts would be beneficial for the establishment of new and enhanced Japanese public diplomacy directions in the future.

In line with this, to explore the insufficient points and less explored areas of Japanese soft power in Europe, the author conducted qualitative personal interviews with French and Bulgarian representatives in the two countries. Based on the findings, the study provided a framework of suggestions with regards to Japan's future cultural projects in France and Bulgaria, conducted both autonomously by the Japan Foundation and in cooperation with various actors and institutions. The Public-Private Partnership Platform was indicated as an essential factor for the organization and implementation of the projects. For maximizing the efficiency of the proposed initiatives, such an integrated approach of close collaboration and coordination between the actors from the public and private sectors is crucial.

Finally, the study discussed certain limitations of the Japan Foundation that should be addressed for further expanding its potential as a major public diplomacy actor in Europe. This included the significance of establishing the Foundation's cultural institutes and/or offices in East European countries. Another issue was the necessity for cooperation to clearly separate activities that currently overlap between the Japan Foundation, the Agency for Cultural Affairs, and other institutions in Europe. Essential for the achievement of such collaboration could be the Public-Private Partnership Platform emphasized previously. It would provide opportunities for the Japan Foundation and those actors to coordinate their projects, enhance their efficiency, and economize funds spent on similar initiatives. Finally, the study revealed the importance for the Japan Foundation to create a system that would clearly explain the efficacy of its projects implemented worldwide.

In conclusion, to increase Japanese soft power in France and Bulgaria, the exercise of integrated public diplomacy through public-private partnerships facilitated by the Japan Foundation is vital. This Public-Private Partnership Platform could also be utilized as a framework of further systemic initiatives for the Japan Foundation both autonomously and in cooperation with Japanese and local institutions in other European countries and worldwide. At the same time, the Foundation should work on its limitations in order to further improve its capacity and potential as Japan's leading public diplomacy actor.

References

Agency for Cultural Affairs. (n.d.). *Cultural exchange and international contributions*. Retrieved August 18, 2018, from www.bunka.go.jp/english/policy/international/

Aniventure. (2019a). *Za Aniventure* [About Aniventure]. Retrieved August 21, 2019, from https://aniventure.net/bg/info/about-aniventure

Aniventure. (2019b). *About Aniventure*. Retrieved February 24, 2019, from https://aniventure.net/en/info/about-aniventure

Belouad, C. (2014). Léon de Rosny, pioneer des études japonaises en France, et ses activités de présentation de la litérature et de la culture japonaises [Leon de Rosny, pioneer of Japanese studies in France, and his activities of presentation of Japanese literature and culture]. In Y. Ishige, T. Kashiwagi, & N. Kobayashi (Eds.), *Les échanges culturels entre le Japon et la France: autour de la collection japonaise d'Emmanuel Tronquois* [Cultural exchanges between Japan and France: Around the Japanese collection of Emmanuel Tronquois] (pp. 215–242). Kyoto: Shibunkaku Shuppan.

Cabinet Office. (2015). *The Cool Japan Public-Private Partnership Platform*. Cool Japan Strategy. Retrieved May 9, 2020, from www.cao.go.jp/cool_japan/english/platform_en/platform_en.html

Cabinet Office. (2018). *Nihon-Gatari-Sho*. Cool Japan Strategy. Retrieved June 6, 2020, from www.cao.go.jp/cool_japan/english/report_en/report_en.html

Chado Urasenke Tankokai, Bulgaria. (n.d.). *Chado Urasenke Tankokai Bulgaria*. Retrieved February 24, 2019, from www.urasenke-bulgaria.net/?inc=page&id=189&s_id=1&lang=en

Cool Japan Fund Inc. (2018). *What is Cool Japan Fund?* Retrieved August 18, 2018, from www.cj-fund.co.jp/en/about/cjfund.html

Cool Japan Movement Promotion Council. (2014). *Cool Japan proposal*. Cabinet Office. Retrieved August 17, 2018 from www.cao.go.jp/cool_japan/english/pdf/published_document3.pdf

Cool Japan Strategy Promotion Council. (2015, June 17). *Cool Japan strategy public-private collaboration initiative*. Retrieved from www.cao.go.jp/cool_japan/english/pdf/published_document2.pdf

Cull, N. J. (2009a). Public diplomacy before gullion: The evolution of a phase. In N. Snow & P. M. Taylor (Eds.), *Routledge handbook of public diplomacy* (pp. 19–23). New York, NY and London: Routledge.

Cull, N. J. (2009b). *Public diplomacy: Lessons from the past.* Los Angeles, CA: Figueroa Press.

Duchâtel, M. (2015, December 7). *The new Japan paradox.* European Council on Foreign Relations. Retrieved August 20, 2018, from www.ecfr.eu/article/ commentary_the_new_japan_paradox5044

Embassy of Japan in Bulgaria. (n.d.-a). Kulturen Obmen [Cultural exchange]. *Dvustranni otnosheniya* [Bilateral relations]. Retrieved December 28, 2019, from www.bg.emb-japan.go.jp/bg/bg_jap_relations/culture_exchange/index.html

Embassy of Japan in Bulgaria. (n.d.-b). Obshta Informatsiya [General information]. *Dvustranni otnosheniya* [Bilateral relations]. Retrieved November 19, 2017, from www.bg.emb-japan.go.jp/itpr_bg/bg_jap_relations.html

Embassy of Japan in Bulgaria. (n.d.-c). *Reisen shūryō-ji made no Burugaria to Nihon no gaikō* [Bulgarian-Japanese relations until the end of the Cold War]. Retrieved November 16, 2020, from www.bg.emb-japan.go.jp/jp/downloads/ nihontomonokai_lecture_ivanov.pdf

Encyclopedia of Art History. (n.d.). Japonism. *Encyclopedia of Art History*. Retrieved January 29, 2019, from www.visual-arts-cork.com/history-of-art/japonism.htm

European Regional Development Fund. (2017). Handbook on Public-Private Partnership (PPP) in Built Heritage Revitalisation Projects. *RESTAURA. Interreg Central Europe.* Retrieved from www.interreg-central.eu/Content.Node/O.T1.1-Handbook-new.pdf

European Union. (n.d.). *Influence of culture on social development through public and private partnership.* Culture & Creativity EU-Eastern Partnership Programme. Retrieved September 29, 2020, from www.culturepartnership.eu/ upload/editor/2017/Factsheets/pdf-12/12_Influence%20of%20culture%20 on%20social%20development.%20Public%20and%20private%20partnership_ ENG.pdf

Fondation Franco-Japonaise Sasakawa. (n.d.). *Présentation de la Fondation* [Presentation of the foundation]. Retrieved February 13, 2019, from http://ffjs.org/ decouvrir/?lang=fr

Genov, G. (2014). *Diplomatsiyata na XXI vek* [The diplomacy of XXI century]. Sofia: Balkan Analytica.

Green, H. (2015). The soft power of cool: Economy, culture and foreign policy in Japan. *Toyo University Repository for Academic Resources, 58*(2), 46–68.

Intellectual Property Strategy Headquarters. (2011, June 3). *Intellectual property strategic program 2011.* Retrieved August 18, 2018, from www.kantei.go.jp/jp/ singi/titeki2/ipsp2011.pdf

Japan Expo. (2018). *France – Japan: A longstanding affinity.* SEFA Event. Retrieved January 29, 2019, from www.japan-expo-paris.com/en/menu_info/ introduction_100984.htm

Japan House. (n.d.). *What is Japan House?* Retrieved August 24, 2019, from www.japanhouselondon.uk/about/what-is-japan-house/

Japan National Tourism Organization. (n.d.). *About JNTO*. Retrieved August 18, 2018, from www.japan.travel/en/about-jnto/

Japan Science and Technology Agency France, PARIS Office. (n.d.). *About us*. Retrieved February 12, 2019, from www.jst.go.jp/inter/paris/JST_About_UK.html

Japan Society for the Promotion of Science. (n.d.). *About us*. Retrieved February 12, 2019, from www.jsps.go.jp/english/aboutus/index2.html

Japan Tourism Agency. (n.d.). *About the JTA*. Retrieved August 18, 2018, from www.mlit.go.jp/kankocho/en/about/index.html

Japonismes 2018. (2018a). *Japonismes 2018: les âmes en resonance* [Japonismes 2018: Souls in resonance]. Retrieved from https://japonismes.org/en/about#background

Japonismes 2018. (2018b). *Japonismes 2018 – Framework*. Retrieved from https://japonismes.org/wp-content/uploads/2018/04/framework.pdf

JSPS Strasbourg office. (n.d.). *Activités* [Activities]. Retrieved February 12, 2019, from http://jsps.unistra.fr/activites/

Kandilarov, E. (2009). *Bulgariya i Yaponiya. Ot Studenata voina kum XXI vek* [Bulgaria and Japan: From the Cold War towards the 21st century]. Sofia: D. Yakov.

Kandilarov, E. (2012). Lyudmila Zhivkova i kulturnata diplomatsiya kum Yaponiya [Lyudmila Zhivkova and the cultural diplomacy towards Japan]. *Novo Vreme, 11*, 89–102.

Kandilarov, E. (2016). *Iztochna Azia I Bulgaria* [East Asia and Bulgaria]. Sofia: Iztok-Zapad.

Kaneko, M. (2007). Nihon no Paburikku Dipuromashi [Japanese public diplomacy]. In M. Kaneko & M. Kitano (Eds.), *Paburikku Dipuromashi* [Public diplomacy] (pp. 184–230). Tokyo: PHP Interface.

Kaneko, M., & Kitano, M. (2014). *Paburikku Dipuromashī Senryaku: Imēji wo Kisou Kokka-kan Gēmu ni Ikani Shōrisuruka* [Public diplomacy strategy: How to win an interstate game competing for images]. PHP Kenkyuusho.

Kinki Bureau of Economy, Trade and Industry. (2018). *Challenge local Cool Japan in Pari* [Challenge local Cool Japan in Paris]. Retrieved February 21, 2019, from www.kansai.meti.go.jp/3-2sashitsu/CCkansai/france/challenge2/sentei.html

Kitera, M. (2018). Présentation de l'Ambassadeur [Presentation of the Ambassador]. *Ambassade du Japon en France* [Embassy of Japan in France]. Retrieved February 13, 2019, from www.fr.emb-japan.go.jp/itpr_fr/presentation-ambassadeur.html

Kokusaikōryūkikin 30-nen hensan-shitsu [The editing room for the history of the Japan Foundation in the past 30 years]. (2006). *Kokusaikōryūkikin 30-nen no Ayumi* [The history of the Japan Foundation in the past 30 years]. Tokyo: The Japan Foundation.

Koleva, E. (2016). Novi metodi v prepodavaneto na yaponski ezik [New teaching methods of Japanese language]. In P. Gergana, A. Andreev, E. Koleva, & A. Todorova (Eds.), *Japan – Times, spirituality and perspectives* (pp. 238–247). Sofia: Universitetsko izdatelstvo "Sv. Kliment Ohridski".

Lacambre, G. (1983). Japonisme [Japanism]. In *Les Arts décoratifs (France)* [Decorative Arts (France)], *France. Délégation aux arts plastiques* [France. Delegation of Plastic Arts], *Musée des arts décoratifs (Paris)* [Museum of Decorative Arts], *Le Livre des expositions universelles, 1851–1989: [exposition, Paris, Musée des arts décoratifs, juin-12 décembre 1983]/[organisée par l'Union centrale des arts décoratifs]; [avec le concours du Ministère de la culture, Délégation aux arts plastiques]* [The book of world expositions, 1851–1989: [exposition, Paris, Museum of Decorative Arts, June–December 12, 1983]/organized by the Central Union of Decorative Arts]; [with the assistance of the Ministry of Culture, Delegation of Plastic Arts] (pp. 297–304). Paris: Éditions des arts décoratifs [Decorative Arts Editions] and Paris: Herscher.

Lavallée, G. (2018, July 15). France goes big on Japan with multi-million cultural program. *Rappler*. Retrieved from www.rappler.com/world/regions/europe/207213-france-japan-multi-million-cultural-program

Le Cordon Bleu. (n.d.). *Japanese cuisine bursary programme*. Retrieved February 20, 2019, from www.cordonbleu.edu/news/japanese-cuisine-bursary-programme/en

Leonard, M., Stead, C., & Smewing, C. (2002). *Public diplomacy*. London: The Foreign Policy Centre.

Maison de la culture du Japon à Paris. (2019). *La MCJP en quelques mots* [The MCJP in a few words]. Retrieved January 31, 2019, from www.mcjp.fr/fr/la-mcjp/presentation

Manga Café. (2018). *A propos* [About]. Retrieved February 18, 2019, from www.mangacafe.fr/a-propos/

Mark, S. (2009). *A greater role for cultural diplomacy* (Discussion papers in diplomacy). The Hague: Netherlands Institute of International Relations 'Clingendael'.

McClellan, M. (2004, October 14). *Public diplomacy in the context of traditional diplomacy*. Retrieved from www.publicdiplomacy.org/45.htm

McGray, D. (2002, May/June). Japan's gross national cool. *Foreign Policy*, pp. 44–54. Retrieved from http://web.mit.edu/condry/Public/cooljapan/Feb23-2006/McGray-02-GNCool.pdf

Melissen, J. (2005a). *Wielding soft power: The new public diplomacy* (Clingendael Diplomacy Papers No. 2). The Hague: Netherlands Institute of International Relations Clingendael.

Melissen, J. (2005b). The new public diplomacy: Between theory and practice. In J. Melissen (Ed.), *The new public diplomacy: Soft power in international relations* (pp. 3–27). London: Palgrave Macmillan.

Minister in Charge of the "Cool Japan" Strategy. (2014). *Declaration of Cool Japan's mission: Japan, a country providing creative solutions to the world's challenges*. Retrieved August 16, 2018, from www.cao.go.jp/cool_japan/english/pdf/published_document4.pdf

Ministry of Economy, Trade and Industry. (2014). *Cool Japan initiative*. Retrieved August 18, 2018, from www.meti.go.jp/policy/mono_info_service/mono/creative/file/1406CoolJapanInitiative.pdf

Ministry of Economy, Trade and Industry. (n.d.). *Japanese food culture promotion project in France*. Retrieved February 19, 2019, from www.meti.go.jp/english/policy/mono_info_service/creative_industries/pdf/130201_01n.pdf

Ministry of Foreign Affairs of Japan. (2014a, August 14). *Public diplomacy: Cultural exchange*. Retrieved August 2, 2018, from www.mofa.go.jp/policy/culture/exchange/index.html

Ministry of Foreign Affairs of Japan. (2014b). *Japan international MANGA award*. Retrieved February, 18, 2019, from www.manga-award.mofa.go.jp/index_e.html

Ministry of Foreign Affairs of Japan. (2014c). *About the MANGA award*. Japan International MANGA Award. Retrieved February, 18, 2019, from www.manga-award.mofa.go.jp/contents/whats_e.html

Ministry of Foreign Affairs of Japan. (2017a). *Diplomatic Bluebook 2017: Japan's foreign policy to promote national and worldwide interests*. Retrieved from www.mofa.go.jp/policy/other/bluebook/2017/html/chapter3/c030402.html

Ministry of Foreign Affairs of Japan. (2017b, July 11). *Public diplomacy: Public relations abroad*. Retrieved August 2, 2018, from www.mofa.go.jp/p_pd/pds/page24e_000149.html

Ministry of Foreign Affairs of Japan. (2018, January 14). *Japan-Bulgaria Relations: Japan-Bulgaria expanded summit meeting and summit dinner meeting*. Retrieved from www.mofa.go.jp/erp/c_see/bg/page1e_000200.html

Ministry of Foreign Affairs of Japan. (2019a). *Diplomatic Bluebook 2019: Japan's foreign policy to promote national and global interests*. Retrieved from www.mofa.go.jp/policy/other/bluebook/2019/html/chapter3/c030402.html

Ministry of Foreign Affairs of Japan. (2019b, February 27). *Press conference by foreign press secretary Takeshi Osuga*. Retrieved from www.mofa.go.jp/press/kaiken/kaiken4e_000612.html

Ministry of Foreign Affairs of Japan. (2020, August 27). *Japan-France relations (basic data)*. Retrieved January 31, 2019, from www.mofa.go.jp/region/europe/france/data.html

Mori, S. (2006). *Japan's public diplomacy and regional integration in East Asia: Using Japan's soft power* (USJP Occasional Paper 06–10). Cambridge, MA: Program on US-Japan Relations, Harvard University.

National Diet Library, Japan. (n.d.). *Section 1: Cuisine. Modern Japan and France – adoration, encounter and interaction*. Retrieved February 19, 2019, from www.ndl.go.jp/france/en/column/s2_1.html

Nye, J., Jr. (2004). *Soft power: The means to success in world politics*. New York, NY: PublicAffairs.

Nye, J., Jr. (2011). *The future of power*. New York, NY: PublicAffairs.

Ogawa, T. (2009). Origin and development of Japan's public diplomacy. In N. Snow & P. M. Taylor (Eds.), *Routledge handbook of public diplomacy* (pp. 270–281). New York, NY and London: Routledge.

Ogoura, K. (2009). *Japan's cultural diplomacy, past and present*. Tokyo: Joint Research Institute for International Peace and Culture, Aoyama Gakuin University, pp. 44–54.

Petkova, G. (2012). Promotion and reception of Japanese culture in Bulgaria. *Seijo CJS Reports*, no. 1. Tokyo: Center for Glocal Studies, Seijo University.

Portland (n.d.). What is soft power? *The Soft Power 30*. Retrieved November 25, 2020, from https://softpower30.com/what-is-soft-power/

Simova, N., & Katrandjiev, V. (2014). *The inter-professional dimension of modern diplomacy*. Sofia: Diplomatic Institute, Ministry of Foreign Affairs Republic of Bulgaria, pp. 134–146.

St. Cyril and St. Methodius International Foundation. (n.d.). *Major programs and activities*. Retrieved February 24, 2019, from www.cmfnd.org/?page_id=1529

The Editors of Encyclopaedia Britannica. (n.d.). Unequal treaty, Chinese history. *Encyclopaedia Britannica Online*. Retrieved August 21, 2021, from www.britannica.com/event/Unequal-Treaty

The Japan Foundation. (2003). *Organization*. Retrieved from www.jpf.go.jp/e/about/result/ar/2003/pdf/ar2003-03-01.pdf

The Japan Foundation. (2015). *Brochure "The Japan Foundation"*. Retrieved from www.jpf.go.jp/e/about/outline/img/Pamphlet_e.pdf

The Japan Foundation. (n.d.). *About us*. Retrieved August 2, 2018, from www.jpf.go.jp/e/about/index.html

U.S. Advisory Commission on Public Diplomacy. (2005). *Cultural diplomacy: The linchpin of public diplomacy* (Report of the Advisory Committee on Cultural Diplomacy). Washington, DC: U.S. Department of State.

USC Center on Public Diplomacy. (n.d.). *What is public diplomacy?* Retrieved August 20, 2021, from http://uscpublicdiplomacy.org/page/what-pd

Vutova-Stefanova, V. (2016). Bulariya-Yaponiya, Dialog i obmen mejdu dve kulturi [Bulgaria-Japan, dialogue and exchange between two cultures]. In P. Gergana, A. Andreev, E. Koleva, & A. Todorova (Eds.), *Japan – Times, spirituality and perspectives* (pp. 137–169). Sofia: Universitetsko izdatelstvo "Sv. Kliment Ohridski".

Wakaba Association. (2019). *Matsuri*. Retrieved February 13, 2019, from www.association-wakaba.com/?-Matsuri-

Walker, C., & Ludwig, J. (2017). *Sharp power, rising authoritarian influence: International forum for democratic studies*. Washington, DC: National Endowment for Democracy, pp. 8–25.

Watanabe, H. (2012, April 20). Japan's cultural diplomacy future. *The Diplomat*. Retrieved from https://thediplomat.com/2012/04/japans-cultural-diplomacy-future/

Watanabe, H. (2018a). The new Japonisme: From international cultural exchange to cultural diplomacy – Evaluating the influence of cultural activities on diplomacy. *Discuss Japan, Japan Foreign Policy Forum, Ministry of Foreign Affairs of Japan. Diplomacy*, 50. Retrieved from www.japanpolicyforum.jp/diplomacy/pt201810301300038356.html

Watanabe, H. (2018b). The 160th anniversary of Franco-Japanese diplomatic relations: How France discovered Japonisme. *Discuss Japan, Japan Foreign Policy Forum, Ministry of Foreign Affairs of Japan, Diplomacy*, 49. Retrieved from www.japanpolicyforum.jp/pdf/2018/no49/DJweb_49_dip_03.pdf

ZOOM Japon. (n.d.). *A propos* [About]. Retrieved February 1, 2019, from http://zoomjapon.info/apropos/

Index

www.ingramcontent.com/pod-product-compliance
Ingram Content Group UK Ltd.
Pitfield, Milton Keynes, MK11 3LW, UK
UKHW020424010325

9 781032 193540